NATIONAL GOALS AND EDUCATION

By

Ismail Thamarasseri

Assistant Professor

Department of Education

Central University of Kashmir

Srinagar - 190 004

(J&K) (INDIA)

DISCOVERY PUBLISHING HOUSE PVT. LTD.

NEW DELHI-110 002

Published by:

Tilak Wasan

DISCOVERY PUBLISHING HOUSE PVT. LTD.
4383/4B, Ansari Road, Darya Ganj
New Delhi-110 002 (India)
Phone : +91-11-23279245, 43596064-65
Fax : +91-11-23253475
E-mail : discoverypublishinghouse@gmail.com
sales@discoverypublishinggroup.com
parul.wasan@gmail.com
web : www.discoverypublishinggroup.com

***First Edition:* 2014**

ISBN: 978-93-5056-454-7

National Goals and Education

Printed at:
Dynamic Printers
Delhi

Foreward

The primary *purpose* of education is to increase the intelligence of young people by helping them develop their potential intelligence into actualised intelligence, thereby contributing to the intelligence capital of a nation. Education has immense *potentiality* to aim at such transferable capacities of the mind that would contribute to the wealth of a nation. It is necessary to explore the concept of knowledge capital as an inevitable ingredient in the pursuit of increasing products or the services. Unless the acquired knowledge is put into practice for the development of the society or country, the efforts and money spent on the education is futile.

I understand it is very much useful to recognise that education has not only purpose, potentiality but *responsibility* to develop philosophical temper, the mindset that accompanies philosophical enquiry, historical temper and the mindset that accompanies historical inquiry as important traits of the educated mind. Education also has another responsibility to develop scientific temper the mindset that accompanies scientific enquiry and social temper, the mindset that accompanies social inquiry, needed for building a better society. Since philosophical, historical, scientific and social inquiries are all forms of rational inquiry, I will focus on what these different tempers have in common, namely, the rational temper. At the core of rational temper is a commitment to the canons of rational inquiry, together with a predisposition to follow them in our professional, public, and personal lives.

The core idea has discussed by the author in various units of this book *'National Goals and Education'* lead to an obvious core rational temper which in turn leads to rational inquiry to build a better nation. The author has discussed in length about the need of the study of Indian constitution, fundamental rights and duties of the citizens, constitutional provisions of primary and higher education. The author has also discussed about the need of secular education, exclusion and inclusion of educational development in India and need of the education for differently abled people.

'National Goals and Education' is designed to acquaint students and scholars with various educational aspects and vast array of information sources available in education. The book describes the purpose, potentiality and responsibility of education. This book provides the comprehensive overview of the necessary of 'citizen education' that gives the harmony of democratic India.

Dr. K. John Babu
Asst. Professor (Convergent Journalism)
Central University of Kashmir
Srinagar
J&K

Preface

Education is a critical input in human resource development and is essential for the country's economic and social growth. Though the major indicators of socio-economic development *viz.*, the growth rate of the economy, birth rate, death rate, infant mortality rate (IMR) and literacy rate, are all inter-connected, the literacy rate and education has been the major determinant of the rise or fall in the other indicators. Prior to 1947, education in India was conducted according to the educational system introduced by the British Government. By Government of India Act (1935) autonomous administration had come in to existence. It was at this time that education was given certain constitutional provisions. In 1944 after the victory of the Allies in the World War II, the British administration once again turned its attention to the development of education in the post-war period. After winning independence, the problem of developing education confronted us. The education ministries of the states and the government of India devoted their best thought to facing the problem. On January 26, 1950, the people of India faithfully dedicated their constitution of themselves. Various provisions have been made for education in the constitution itself. Education has always been accorded an honored place in Indian society. The great leaders of the Indian freedom movement realised the fundamental role of education and throughout the nation's struggle for independence, stressed its unique significance for national development. Mahatma Gandhi formulated the scheme of Basic Education seeking to harmonize intellectual and manual work. This was a great step forward in making education directly relevant to the life of the people. Many other national leaders likewise made important contributions to national education before independence.

This book discussing the ideals, values and national goals of education in Indian context. This book comprehensively covers the different aspects of national goals and education. This book is useful for students of education *i.e.*, B.Ed., M.Ed., M.A. (Education) in particular and those who interested in the area of Indian Education in general. In preparation of this book the author had to refer to the works of other authors and information sources. The author feel a deep sense of gratitude for incorporating their ideas in the text. The author extremely indebted to various authors, editors, educationists, technologists and research scholars, whose views and opinions have been incorporated in this book. The author grateful to his colleagues, friends, family members and students whose offered suggestions, guidance and assistance. Finally, the author whole heartedly expresses his indebtedness to M/s. Discovery Publishing House Pvt Ltd. for the meticulous process and publishing of the work. Moreover, all the suggestions and comments are invited for the further improvement of the work.

Ismail Thamarasseri

Contents

Pre-amble of Indian Constitution

The preamble of the constitution is described as an identity card of the constitution. It contains the 'epitome' of the objectives to which the people of a country are permanently committed.

The preamble to the constitution of India summarises its aim and objectives. It reads as follows:

We the people of India, having solemnly resolved to constitute India into a Sovereign Socialist Secular Democratic Republic and to secure to all its citizens.

- *Justice*, Social-economic political.
- *Liberty* of thought, expression, belief, faith and worship.
- *Equality* of status and of opportunity, and promote among them all.
- *Fraternity* assuring the dignity of the individual and the unity and integrity of the nation.

In our Constituent Assemblythis 26th day of November, 1949 do hereby adopt, Enact and Give to Ourselves this constitution.

Note: Three new terms-socialist, secular and integrity were added to the original text of the preamble when in 1976 the government passed the 42nd Amendment.

Education in the concurrent list – Till 1976 education was a state subject but with the 42nd Amendment to the constitution which received the president's assent on December 18, 1976, It was put on concurrent list.

Entry 25 of the concurrent list includes, "Education, including technical education, medical education and universities subject to entries 63, 64, 66 of list 1, vocational and technical training of labour".

The Significance of Preamble of Indian Constitution

The preamble of constitution of India prescribes that the people of the country would try to secure.

1. Social, economic and political justice.
2. Liberty of thought, expression, belief, faith and worship.
3. Equality of status and of opportunity.
4. A sense of fraternity to assure the dignity of the individual and the unity of the nation.

Importance of the Preamble

Even preamble is not the part of constitution it has special significance. It sets forth the source from which the constitution draws its inspiration. It shows that the authority originates from the people of India. No individual or a class of individuals can claim to be the source of authority in India. The Government of India must be carried on by the elected representatives of the people. The head of the state must be an elected president. It can help the judges to understand the general objects and intentions of the constitution or of any law, which has been passed under that provision.

Conclusion

Here we can conclude that taking the rights guaranteed under religious, educational and cultural field as a whole, it will be noted that these are conched in the most comprehensive language and the maximum possible freedom is guaranteed to the minorities, religious and linguistics. The democratic basis of the constitution would have been lost if the minorities were not given adequate protection to preserve their religious beliefs, and institutions of education and culture.

REFERENCES

1. Ismail Thamarasseri (2007), *Education in the Emerging Indian Society*. New Delhi: Kanishka Publishers.

2

Education as a Fundamental Right

In order to fulfill the obligations enshrined in the preamble of the constitution, provisions are made in it in the form of article and the corresponding clauses. The various constitutional provisions regarding education in India are in accordance with our political, economic and cultural needs. These provisions regarding education in India aim at fulfilling the aspirations of the people through the medium of education. The constitution of India provides the following provisions relating to education in the country.

- *Article 45:* Article 45 states, "The state shall endeavour to provide with in a period of ten years from the commencement of this constitution, for free and compulsory education for all children until they complete the age of fourteen years".

Article 45 of directive principles of state policy includes the most important constitutional provision regarding Indian Education. It deals with free and compulsory primary education.

Baroda, a tiny state of India, introduced compulsory primary education in 1906. In 1911, Mr. Gopala Krishna

Gokhale, a member of Imperial Legislature, moved a resolution in the council to make elementary education free and compulsory throughout the country, but it was rejected. It became reality in 1920 when all the provisional governments passed acts for introducing compulsory primary education in their provinces. Gandhiji's Scheme of basic education (1937) also aimed at providing primary education to all children until they completed the age of 14 years. The Sargent report also recommended a universal system of primary education.

The Norms of Fundamental Right of Education

1. Provision of teachers in the ratio of 1:30 at primary and upper primary level and a provision of at least two teachers in every two primary schools.
2. Provision of a upper primary school for every two primary schools. This would entail establishment of more than 2.21 lack new upper primary schools.
3. Provision of primary school within one km., of every habitation. This would entail the establishment of nearly 1.84 lakh new primary schools.
4. Provision of classroom for every teacher and a separate Headmaster's room in upper primary school.
5. Provision of schools equipments to add proposed new primary schools and upper primary schools as per the operation blackboards norm of Rs. 10,000 per primary schools and Rs. 50,000 per upper primary school.
6. Provision for school uniform and scholarship to children below the poverty line. Provisions has been made for 50 per cent add the enrolled children in the 6-14 age group.
7. Provision of cooked meal/food grains to 50 per cent of the enrolled children which has been made though the final figure should be based on actual requirement and livelihood of success of the scheme.
8. Provision of free text books and stationary has been made for all the children at primary and upper primary levels as per norms given by the NCERT.

9. Establishment of new DIETS, Block Resource Centres and cluster resources centres have been made in uncovered regions.
10. Provisions for maintenance of school buildings and other school infrastructure and replacement of school equipments at primary and upper primary stage have also been made on regular basis.
11. For disabled children, an assessment of four per cent of the total children has been made and provisions made as per current norms in scheme for disabled persons four per cent incidence of disability has been taken on the basis of some current assessment in this regard.
12. Provision for teacher training, and community monitoring of elementary education projects and classroom observation by resource persons has also been made.
13. The 1993, all India educational survey provides basis for assessing educational facilities that were available to schools in 1993. Between 1993 and 1997-98, investments have been made by central and state governments.

Administration

Education was a state subject till 3rd January 1977 when the 22nd amendment to the constitution was made to bring education under concurrent list. The amendment cancelled (deleted) the 'entry' of the state list and enlarged the 'entry 25' in the concurrent list.

The entry 25 of the concurrent list how reads as, "Education, including technical education, medical education and universities subject to the provisions of entries 63, 64, 65 and 66 of list I, vocational and technical training of labour".

List I (Union List)

- *Entry 63:* Universities and other institutions declared by parliament by law to be institutions of national importance.
- *Entry 64:* Institutions for specific or technical education declared by parliament to be institutions of national importance.

- *Entry 65:* Mentions union agencies and institutions for professional, Vocational or technical training for the promotion of special studies or research etc.
- *Entry 66:* The co-ordination and determination of standards in institution for higher education, or research and scientific and technical institutions becomes the exclusive responsibility of the union.

Universal Primary Education

86th Constitutional Amendment (2002) Amending Article 21, 51 (A) and Article 45.

Article 21 (A)

Article 21 states the fundamental rights of Indian citizens. It means that of enables the citizen to seek the enforcement of the right by way of resort to 'write' under Article 32 and 226 of the constitution.

The new Article, Article 21 A says that "the state shall provide free and compulsory education to all children of the age six to fourteen years in such a manner as the state may, by law, determine".

By the 86th constitutional amendment right to education, for children aged between 6 to 14 years had become the right of citizen under Article 21 which can be enforced through law. By this amendment, our 'rights' had increased from 6 to 7.

Article 51A (K)

Article 51A defines the fundamental duties of the citizens. The new clause to Article 51A (K) sates that "It shall be the duty of every citizen of India who is a parent of guardian to provide opportunities for education to his child or as the case may be, ward between the age of six and fourteen years".

Article 45

Article 45 says about education of children under age group 0-6 that is ECCE.

Criticism

Many legal experts, educationalists and voluntary organizations like National Alliance for the Fundamental

Rights to Education (NAFRE) had criticized the amendment. A few most important among them are given below.

(*a*) The Guarantee of education for 6 to 14 years category is meaningless without the state taking responsibility for Early Childhood Care and Education (ECCE). The bill does not address the issue of making ECCE, a concept noted in the NPE, 1986 amendatory without which the complete enrolment of childrens especially of girls education, of the age group 6-14 to primary class will be difficult.

(*b*) According to D. Anil Sadgopal, former Dean and Head of the Department of Education Delhi University, in the amendment, the element of enforcement had been taken out. The amendment is not attached with any financial provision and it shows the governments lack of commitment to the objective.

(*c*) Another feature of the Amendment which is criticized is the insertion of clause 'K' under Article 51A. Under the clause there is a possibility of assment, by the authorities of parents who is not giving opportunities for education to their children due to financial or any such problem in which they have no contrast.

The NAFRE points out that between 1951 to 1971 at least 15 lakhs parents have been prosecuted under the State Compulsory Education Act, which was inforce in 19 states. The meaning of the term 'opportunity for education' is also much criticized.

(*d*) It is also said that the government had diluted the objective of guaranteeing free and Universal Elementary Education (UEE) to all children by keeping 0-6 age group under the directive principles.

REFERENCES

1. Ismail Thamarasseri (2007), *Education in the Emerging Indian Society*. New Delhi: Kanishka Publishers.

Fundamental Rights and Duties of Indian Citizen

Fundamental Rights (Part III Articles 12-35 of Indian Constitution)

Six Broad Categories of Fundamental Rights

1. *The Right to Equality,* including the equality before law and the equal protection of laws (Article 14), prohibition of discrimination on grounds of religion, race, caste, sex or place of birth (Article 15), equality of opportunity in matters of public employment (Article 16) and abolition of untouchability and the system of titles (Article 17, 18).
2. *The Right to Freedom,* including the right to protection of life and personal liberty (21) and the right to freedom of speech and expression, assembly, association or union, movement and reside and settle in any part of India, and the right to practice any profession and occupation (Article 19).

Right to Education

Article 21 (A) added as a new article by the constitution (86th Amendment) Act 2002 provides for free and compulsory education for all children between the age of 6-14 years. This included under right to freedom.

3. *The Right Against Exploitation,* prohibiting all forms of forced labour, child labour and traffic in human beings (Article 23, 24).
4. *The Right to Freedom of Conscience and free Profession,* practice and propagation of religion (Article 25 to 28).
5. *The Right of Minorities to Conserve their Culture,* language and script and to establish and administer educational institutions of their choice (Article 29, 30).
6. *The Right to Constitutional Remedies for the Enforcement of all these Fundamental Rights* (Article 32).

Education as Fundamental Right

The conflict between man and the state is as old as human history. Although attempts have been made for centuries to bring about a proper adjustment between the competing claims of the state and the individual, the solution seems to be still far off. This is primarily because of the dynamic nature of human society where old values, ideas and forces constantly yield place to new ones. It is obvious that if individuals are allowed to have absolute freedom of speech and action, the result would be chaos, ruin and anarchy. Hence, the eternal problem that faced statesman and political scientists was how to make a proper adjustment between individual freedom and social control, the need for protecting personal liberty against governmental power and that of limiting personal liberty by governmental power. The problem assumes extreme difficulty only under a democratic system of government. A democracy aims at the maximum development of the individual's personality; and the personality of the individual is inseparably boand with his liberty. Only a free society can assure the progress of its members which ultimately helps the advancement of human welfare. Therefore, every democracy pays special attention to securing this basic objective to the maximum extent without, at the same time, endangering the security of the state itself. A common device that is adopted by most of them for this purpose is to incorporate a list of fundamental rights in their constitutions and guarantee them from violation by executive and legislative authorities. The theory of fundamental rights implies limited government.

The provisions of Part III of our constitution which enumerates the Fundamental Rights are more elaborate than those of any other Fundamental Rights, and cover a wide range of topics. The constitution itself classifies the fundamental rights under seven groups as follows:

1. Right to equality.
2. Right to particular freedom.
3. Right against exploitation.
4. Right to freedom of religion.
5. Cultural and educational rights.
6. Right to property (eliminated by 44th Amendment Act).
7. Right to constitutional remedies.

Fundamental Duties of Indian Citizen

(Part IV A - Article 51. A)

It is one of the valuable part of constitution and also most neglected.

The fundamental duties enshrined in article 51(A) now are in consonance with article 29(1) of the Universal Declaration of Human Rights which says: "every one has duties to the community in which alone the free and full development of his personality is possible".

The new part IV. A, articles 51 A (a) to (j) laid down to constitution (86th amendment) Act 2002 added new clause (K) as the eleventh duty.

1. **To Abide by the Constitution and Respect its Ideas and Institutions, the National Flag and the National Anthem**

These are the very physical foundations of our citizenship. All of us are supposed to maintain the dignity of the constitution, by not indulging in any activities in violation of the letter of spirit of the constitution. Our is a vast country with many languages, sub-cultures, religions and ethnic diversities, but the essential unity of the country is epistomised in the one constitution, one flag, one people and one citizenship.

We are governed and guided by this constitution irrespective of caste, religion, race, sex etc. We must put the nation above our narrow personal interests and then only we will be able to protect our hard-earned freedom and sovereignty.

2. To Cherish and follow the Noble Ideals which Inspired our National Struggle for Freedom

If we, the citizens of India, remain conscious of and committed to these ideals, we will fissiparous tendencies raising their ugly heads now and there here and there. Parties and politicians who use religion, casteism, separation etc., for political ends and for capturing power are clearly violating their fundamental duties under the constitution.

3. To Uphold and Protest the Sovereignty, Unity and Integrity of India

In a democratic system of governance, sovereignty lies with the people. To defend our sovereignty is our own responsibility. If the freedom and unity of the country are jeoponsibility. If the freedom and unity of the country are jeoparadised, the nation ceases to exist and if there is no nation, who lives?

4. To Defend the Country and Render National Service when called upon to do so

Civilians may be required also to take up arms in defence of the country, if the situation warrants it. By fighting to defend the country, the citizens are fighting only to defend their own liberty and that of their posterity.

5. To Promote Harmony and the Spirit of Common Brother Hood Amongst all the People of India Transcending Religious, Linguistic and Regional or Sectional Diversities to Renounce Practices Derogatory to the Dignity of Women

'Yatra Naristu Pujayan the Ramanthe Thathradevatha', (gods reside where women are worshiped). That's our culture, India is a land diversities, we must keep a unity even the diversities.

6. To Value and Preserve the Rich Heritage of our Composite Culture

One of the most ancient civilizations of the world, India can take legitimate pride in having been a civilizational unity without a break for more than 5000 years. We all are the part of this great civilization and culture. Our contribution in the field of art, sculpture, architecture, mathematics, science, medicine etc., are well known. Some of the oldest, deepest and most sublime philosophical thought and literature was born in India. We have several historical monuments or great archeological value spread over the entire country. These includes forests, palaces, temples etc. As to this territory had the honour of being the birth place of several great religions like Hinduism, Budhism, Jainism and Sikhism. Our past has shown us the path of peace, love, non-violence and truth. As citizens of this country, it is the responsibility of all of us to work for the preservation of this rich heritage and its cultural values and live in love and harmony.

The directive principles under Article 49 similarly enjoins, the state to protect monuments and places and objects of national, artistic or historical importance.

7. To Protect and Improve the Natural Environment Including Forests, Lakes, Rivers and Wild Life to have Compassion for Living Creatures

In the face of menace of the increasing pollution and environmental degradation, it is the duty of every citizen to protect and improve natural environment including, forests, lakes, rivers and wild life and to have compassion for living creatures.

Earth is the common heritage of man and animals. We have no right to annihilate of drive away from their territory or natural habitat or the world denizens. 'Sarveshawam Santhir Bhavanthu' (peace unto all living beings and entire environment), and '*Ahimsaparamodarma, ahimsa parmothapa*' (non-violence is the greatest duty and the greatest penance).

8. To Develop the Scientific Temper, Humanism and Spirit of Inquiry and Reform

One of our great founding fathers, Nehru, always laid great emphasis on the need for Indian citizens developing a scientific temper and a spirit of inquiry-an inquisitiveness for learning from developments around the world. It is the bounden duty of every citizen to preserve and promote a scientific temper and a spirit of inquiry to keep pace with the fast changing world.

9. To Safeguard Public Property and to Abjure Violence

It is most unfortunate that in a country which preaches non-violence to the rest of the world, we see from time to time spectacles of senseless violence and destruction of public property indulged in by a few of its citizens.

10. To Strive Towards Excellence in all Spheres of Individual and Collective Activity, So that the Nation Constantly Rises to Higher Level of Endeavour and Achievement

To drive for excellence in all spheres of individual and collective activity is the demand of times and a basic requirement in a highly competitive world. Nothing, but the best would have survival potential in tomorrow's world. This would include respect for professional obligations and excellence.

11. Every Parent or Guardian to Provide Opportunities for Education to his Child or Ward between the Age of 6-14 Years

The National Commission to Review the Working of the Constitution (NCRWC) had recommended making education a fundamental right for all children up to the age of 14.

The constitution (86th Amendment) Act 2002 however provided for free and compulsory education as a legally enforceable fundamental right for all children between the 6-14 years. To meet the criticism of not covering the children below 6 yeas, the Act amended directive principles to say that the state shall endeavour to provide Early Childhood Care and Education (ECCE) for all children below the age of six years. Also it added a new clause (K) to chapter IV A, Article 51 A to cast on parents and guardians a duty to provide opportunities for education to children between the age 6-14 years.

There is no provision in the constitution for direct enforcement of the fundamental duties enshrined in Article 51 A nor is there any provision to prevent or punish their violation.

The National Commission to Review the Working of the Constitution (2002-02 – NCRWC) [appointed by President of India on 23rd February 2000 and submitted its report on 31 March 2002 – regarding the completion of constitution's 50 years. 1990-2000] recommended the following should be incorporated as fundamental duties in Article 51(A) of the constitution.

1. To foster a spirit of family values and responsible parent hood in the matter of education, physical and moral well-being of children.
2. Duty of industrial organizations to provide education to children of their employees.

REFERENCES

1. Ismail Thamarasseri (2007), *Education in the Emerging Indian Society*. New Delhi: Kanishka Publishers.

Constitutional Provisions on Education

Constitutional Guarantee

Prior to 1947, education in India was conducted according to the educational system introduced by the British Government. By Government of India Act (1935) autonomous administration had come in to existence. It was at this time that education was given certain constitutional provisions. In 1944 after the victory of the Allies in the World War II, the British administration once again turned its attention to the development of education in the post-war period.

After winning independence, the problem of developing education confronted us. The education ministeries of the states and the government of India devoted their best thought to facing the problem. On January 26, 1950, the people of India faithfully dedicated their constitution of themselves. Various provisions have been made for education in the constitution itself.

Article 30: The Right of Minorities to Set Up and Administer Educational Institutions

- *30(1)*: All minorities based on religion or language will have the right to set up and administer institutions in their own interest.

- *30(2)*: In giving aid to educational institutions, the government will not discriminate against any institution on the basis of its being set up and administered by the particular religious or linguistic minority.

The government will not foist any language of its own choice on any minority. The minority status of a group will be determined on the basis of its population. The reservation of particular groups not be considered as a violation of the constitution. No educational institution will be entitled to refuse admission to any child on the basis of religion, caste, creed or language.

Article 45: Provision for Free and Compulsory Education for Children

"The state shall endeavour to provide, within a period of ten years from the commencement of this constitution, for free and compulsory education for all children until they complete the age of fourteen years".

Amendment of the Constitution

The 86th Amendment (2002) inserts a new article 21(A) to provide for a fundamental right to education to all children of 6-14 years. Also, it substitutes article 45 in the directive principles by a new article providing for Early Child Care and Education to children below 6 years. By amending Article 51(A), a new fundamental duty is sought to be added for parents or guardians providing educational opportunities to children between the age of 6-14 years.

Article 46: Promotion of Educational and Economic Interests of the Scheduled Castes, Scheduled Tribes and other weaker Sections

The state shall promote with special care the educational and economic interests of the weaker sections of the people, and in particular, of the scheduled castes and the scheduled tribes, and shall protect them from social injustice and all forms of exploitation.

Article 28: Freedom as to Attendance at Religious Instruction or Religious Worship in Certain Educational Institutions

There are many religions in India, with very substantial numbers of followers. Though our country is itself a secular state, the constitution of our country has shown great awareness or that religious susceptibilities of the people.

- *28(1)*: Any educational institution drawing its total financial assistance from the governments funds must not impart education of any religion.
- *28(2)*: The condition is part (1) shall not applicable to any educational institutions administered by the state but in the case of an institution established by a trust or a religious body, religious education may be carried on.
- *28(3)*: Any educational institution which receives aid from the government funds shall not compel any individual admitted to that institution take part in any religious activities conducted in the institution or any place of worship attached to it, as long as permission to do so has not been obtained from that individual, or if he is a minor from his guardians.

Article 29: Protection of Interests of Minorities

The most controversial part of the Indian constitution.

- *29(1)*: The citizens in any part of the country having their own specific language, script and culture, will have the right to maintain these languages, scripts and cultures.

The article clearly grants to the individual the right choose his own culture and language and it also clarifies that each state and its citizen will be to choose their own language and culture.

- *29(2)*: No citizen shall be denied admission in to educational institution maintained by the state or receiving aid out of state funds on grounds only of religion, race, caste, language or any of them.

Article 27: Freedom as to Payment of Taxes for Promotion of Any Particular Religion

No person shall be compelled to pay any taxes, the proceeds of which are specifically appropriated in payment of expenses for the promotion or maintenance of any particular religion or religious denomination.

Article 350: Language to be used in Representations for Redress of Grievances

Every individual has the right to give representation to an officer in state or central language.

350 (A): Facilities for Instruction in Mother Tongue at Primary Stage

- *350(a)*: Advise that education be imparted in the mother tongue, starting that if will be the endeavour of every state, and of every local official within the state to provide suitable facilities for providing education to the children of linguistic minorities in their mother tongue at the primary stage.

350(B): Special Officer for Linguistic Minorities

- *350(1)*: There will be a special officer appointed by the president of India for linguistic minorities.
- *350 B(2)*: It will be the duty of the special officer to conduct research or studies in to all subjects related to the notion of linguistic minorities as defined in this constitution, and to send suggestions to the president regarding these subjects.

351: Directive for Development of the Hindi Language

It shall be the duty of the union to promote the spread of the Hindi language, to develop it so that it may serve as a medium of expression for all the elements of the composite culture of India and to secure its enrichment by assimilating without interfering with its genius, the forms, style and expressions used in Hindustani and in the other languages of India specified in the eight schedule, and by drawing, wherever necessary/desirable for its vocabulary, primarily on Sanskrit and secondarily on other languages.

Indian Constitution Articles 345, 346, 347 dealing with regional languages.

- *345*: languages used for states purposes.
- *346*: the state language for communication between one state and another or between state and union.

- *347*: special provisions relating to a language spoken by a section of the population of a state.
- *343*: related official language of the union. Hindi in the Devanagri script, and use of international number system.

Education as a Fundamental Rights

21(A) added as a new article by constitution (86th Amendment) Act 2002 provides for free and compulsory education for all children between the age of 6-14 years.

REFERENCES

1. Ismail Thamarasseri (2007), *Education in the Emerging Indian Society*. New Delhi: Kanishka Publishers.

Constitutional Provisions Related to Elementary Education

Introduction

The Indian constitution is the bulkiest written constitution in the world. Our constitution which came into existence on 26th January 1950 consists of 444 articles including sub clauses (originally it has 395 articles) and 24 parts and 12 schedules. As education is an integral part of any country our constitution also provides some provisions to Education. Recently the parliament approved the bill that education as one of the fundamental right, earlier it was in the state list. From 18th December 1976 by the 42nd amendment of the constitution education came under concurrent list.

Constitutional Provisions for Education

The following are the important articles that related to education.

- *Article 21 (A)*: Article 21(A) states the fundamental rights of Indian citizens. The new Article 21(A) says "the state shall provide free and compulsory education to all children of the age six to fourteen years in such a manner as the state may, by law, determine".

- *Article 51 (A)*: Defines the fundamental duties of the citizens. The new clause to Article 51A(K) states that "It shall be the duty of every citizen of India who is parent of guardian to provide opportunities for education to his child or as the case may be, ward between the age of six and fourteen years".
- *Article 25*: "No religious instruction is given in any educational institution".
- *Article 28(i)*: "No religious instruction shall be provided by any educational institution wholly maintained out of states fund".
- *Article 28 (ii)*: "Nothing in clause (1) shall be applied to an educational institution which is administered by the state but has been established under any endowment (OR) trust which requires that religious instruction shall be imparted in that institute".
- *Article 28 (iii)*: "No person attending any educational institution recognised by the state (OR) receiving out of the state fund shall be required to take part in any religious instruction that may be imparted in such institutions (OR) attend any religious worship that may be conducted in such institution (OR) in any premises attached there to unless such person (OR) if such person is a minor his guardian has given his consent there to".
- *Article 29 (i)*: "It provides that any section of citizens residing in the territory of India (OR) any part there of have the freedom to preserve the script (OR) follow any language (OR) culture of its own shall have the right to conserve the same".
- *Article 29 (ii)*: "No citizen shall be denied admission into any educational institution by the state (OR) receiving aid out of the state funds on grounds only of religion, caste, race, language (OR) any one of them".
- *Article 30*: "It states that the state shall not in granting aid to educational institution discriminate against any educational institutions on the grounds that it is under

the management of a minority whether based on religion (OR) language".

- *Article 30(i)*: "All minorities whether based on religion (OR) language shall have the right to establish and administer educational institution of their choice".
- *Article 30 (ii)*: "The state shall not discriminate against any educational institution in respect of granting aid on the ground that it is under the management of minority whether based on religion (OR) language".
- *Article 26 (i)*: "Any section of the citizens residing in the territory of India (OR) any part their of having a distinct language, script (OR) culture of its own shall have the right to converse the same".
- *Article 25 (i)*: "Indian constitution guarantees all the citizens the right to have freedom of conscience and right to profess, practice and propagate any religion".
- *Article 46*: "The state shall promote with special care the education and economic interest of the weaker sections of the people and in particular of the SC/ST and Shall protect them from social injustice and from all forms of exploitations".
- *Article 350 (A)*: "It shall be the endeavour (attempt) of every state and every local authority to provide adequate facilities for instruction in the mother tongue at the primary state of education belonging linguistic minority group".

Education as a Concurrent Subject

The forty-second Amendment 1976 brought about drastic changes in the Indian Constitution. It put education, hitherto a state subject on the concurrent list. The Swaran Singh Committee said 'Agriculture and education are subjects of prime importance to the country's rapid progress towards achieving desired socio-economic objectives. This amendment makes central and state government equal partners in framing educational policies. Union becomes supreme over states in enacting law regarding education. The executive power is given to the union to give direction to the states. The states have powers limited to the extent that there do not impede (OR) prejudice the exercise of the executive powers of the union. The centre can implement directly any policy decision in any state, national institutes like UGC, NCERT and National bodies like CABE have high power and strength to shape the education of the country in all the states.

Universalisation of Elementary Education

Indian had a glorious past: once upon a time cities like Mohanjo Daro and Harappa and ports like Lothal flourished here. Famous physicians and surgeons like Charaka, Sushrutha and Vagabhata lived in this country. Mathematics and astronomy have got important place. From the four conrners of the world scholars came to use to Nalanda and Taxila in search of humanity.

Gone are those days. Today we are the most illiterate nation in the world, the most sick nation in the world, the most hungry nation in the world. Even the very freedom for which our forefathers faught in danger.

We wrote in our constitution (Article 45) that "The state shall endeavour to provide within a period of ten years from the commencement of the constitution for free and compulsory education for all children until they complete the age of 14 years".

Sixty years ago Mahatma Gandhi said "We have the education of this future state. I say without fear of my figures being challenged successfully, that today India is more illiterate than it was fifty (OR) hundred years ago, and so is Burma, because the British administrators when they came to India, instead of taking hold of things as they were, began to root them out.

Status and Achievement of UEE in India

There is no gain saying in stating the fact that a large majority of these million of illiterate and non-enrolled and/or out of school children are residing in South Asia. That is a majority of this population is in India is not only the most embrassing but also the most disturbing aspect of the efforts we have made so far towards achieving the cherished goal of universalization of elementary education. That is not all the unfortunate part of the story is that the country is now here near achieving even the goals of universalisation of primary education. The earlier this stark reality is recognised by one and all in India, the better it will be for all of us – the macro level high profile administrator and the low profile micro level field workers. Resolutions (OR) promulgations of ordinances as well as public clichés are just not going to make an iota in the existing situation *i.e.*, being almost at the bottom of the list of countries in providing basic education for all.

All available information strongly indicates that the time of attainment of independence in 1947, the health and education scenario in the country was, to say the least, dismal, if not altogether hopeless young children and mothers were an utterly neglected lot. The mortality rate was very high and morbidity rampant in the young population due to talk of proper health care and adequate nutrition. The level of achievement in elementary education was extremely low in almost all respects. Thousands of villages and rural habitations, particularly those in hilly and mountainous regions, were without schools. Only one child out of three in the age group 6-11 and one child out of eleven in the age group of 11-14 were enrolled in schools. Educational inequalities were large, especially between one region and another between urban is rural areas between boys and girls and between the advanced and intermediate castes, on the one hand and SC/ST and OBC on the other. The quality of elementary education was poor and the rates of drop-out and stagnation were extremely high.

India undertook the gigantic task of national construction aimed at bringing about socio-economic transformation and at creating a new social order based on the principles of democracy, social-justice and secularism. That without providing education to masses, it was well high impossible to achieve economic development and to establish a just and egalitarian society, came to be accepted as an indisputable fact by those who frame the Indian constitution. Hence the total commitment to making the provision of free and compulsory education for all children in the age group 06-14. This cherished goal should have been attained by the year 1960. However, this target date had to be first revised to 1970 then to 1976 and later to 1988. The new target date according to the resolution in the National Policy on Education 1986. One would wish that as a nation we should have been more discreet in fixing the target which were realistic and within our reach.

73rd and 74th Constitutional Amendments and their Implications for Elementary Education

Though the Panchayath Raj Institutions have been in existence for a long time, it has been observed that these institutions have not been able to acquire the status and dignity of variable and responsible people's bodies due to a number of reasons including absence of regular elections, prolonged supersessions, in sufficient representation of weaker sections like SC/ST and women, inadequate devolution of powers and lack of financial resources.

Article 40 of the constitution, which enshrines one of the directive principle of state policy lays down that the state shall take steps to organize village panchayats and rest them with such powers and authority as may as necessary to enable them to function as units of self-government. In the light of the experience of the last 50 years and in view of the short-comings, which have been observed it is considered that there is an imperative need to enshrine in the constitution certain basic and essential features of Panchayat Raj institutions to impart certainly, continuity and strength to them.

A Grama Sabha is empowered to exercise such powers and perform such functions at village level as the legislature of a state may by law provide article 243A.

Article 243B provides for the constitution of Panchayats at the village, intermediate and district levels. However Panchayats at the intermediate level may not be constituted in a state where population does not exceed twenty lakhs.

Legislature of a state is empowered to make provisions with regard to composition of panchayats provided that the ratio between the population of the territorial area of the panchayat at any level and the member of seats in such panchayat to be filled by election shall be same through out the state.

The chairperson of a panchayat at the village level shall be elected in such manner as the legislative of a state may by law, provide and a panchayat at the intermediate level (OR) district level shall be elected by and from amongst, the elected members thereof 243D provides for reservation of seats and offices of chairpersons to the SC/ST and women and women belonging to the SC/ST.

The duration of every panchayat shall be five years (Article 243E) 243 F provides for disqualification for being chosen as and for being a member of Parliament if he is disqualified to contest the elections to the legislature of the state concerned. Provided no person shall be qualified to contest the election if he is less than twenty five years of age if he has attained the age of twenty one years.

The provisions of the newly inserted part IX of the constitution (73rd Amendment) Act 1993 shall apply to the Union Territories provides that the president is empowered to direct that the provisions of this part shall apply to any Union Territory (OR) part there of subject to the subject exceptions and modifications as he may specify in the notification.

In many states local bodies have become weak and ineffective on account of a variety of reasons, including the failure to hold regular elections, prolonged suppressions and inadequate devolution of powers and functions. As a result, urban and local bodies are not able to perform effectively as vibrant democratic units of self-government.

Having regard to these inadequacies, it was considered necessary that provisions relating to urban local bodies are incorporated in the constitution particularly, for –

(i) Putting on a firmer footing the relationship between the state government and the urban local bodies with respect to:

(a) the functions and taxation powers; and

(b) arrangements for revenue sharing.

(ii) Ensuring regular conduct of election.

(iii) Ensuring timely elections in the case of supersessions.

(iv) Providing adequate representation for the weaker sections and SC/ST and women.

Accordingly, it has been proposed to add a new part relating to the urban local bodies in the constitution to provide for –

(a) The constitution of three types of municipalities.

(b) Composition of municipalities, which will be decided by the legislature of state.

(i) Representation of chairperson of committees, if any at ward (OR) other levels in the municipalities.

(c) Election of chairperson of a municipality in the manner specified in the state of law.

(d) Constitution of committees at ward level (OR) other level (OR) levels within the territorial area of a municipality as may be provided in the state of law.

(e) Reservation of seats in every municipality –

(i) for SC/ST in proposition to their population of which not less than one third shall be for women.

(ii) For women which shall not be less than one third of the total number of seats.

(iii) In favour of backward class of citizens if so provided by the legislature of the state.

(iv) For SC/ST and women in office of chairpersons as may be specified in the state of law.

(f) Fixed tenure of 5 years for the municipality and re-election within a period of six months of its dissolution.

(g) Devolution by the state legislature of powers and responsibilities upon the municipalities with respect to preparation of plans for economic development and social justice and for the implementations of development schemes as may be required to enable them to function as institutions of self-government.

(h) Levy of taxes and duties by municipalities assigning of such taxes and duties to municipalities by state governments and for making grants in aid by the state to the municipalities as may be provided in the state law.

(i) A finance commission to review the finances of the municipalities and to recommend principles for –

1. Determining the taxes which may be assigned to the municipalities.
2. Sharing of taxes between the state and municipalities.
3. Grants-in-aid to the municipalities from the consolidated fund of the state.

(j) audit of accounts of the municipal corporations by the comptroller and Auditor General of India and laying of reports before the legislature of the state and the municipal corporation concerned.

(k) making of law by a state legislature with respect to elections to the municipalities to be conducted under the superintendence, direction and control of the chief election officer of the state.

(i) application of the provisions of the Bill to any Union Territory (OR) part thereof with such modifications as may be specified by the president.

(n) Bar of jurisdiction of courts in matters relating to elections to the municipalities.

Directive Principles in Article 45

Free and Compulsory Primary Education

Article 45, under directive principles of state policy lays down. "The state shall endeavour to provide within a period of ten years from the commencement of this constitution, for free and compulsory education for all children until they complete the age of fourteen years". Now Article 45 also dealt with Early Childhood Care and Education (ECCE).

National and State Policies on Elementary Education

National System of Education

The New Education policy has been designed to see that a national system of education is created and all imbalances and disparities are removed in all sectors of education. The national system is based on a national curriculum framework which contains a common core along with other components that are flexible. The common core includes the history of Indian's freedom movement, our constitutional obligations, our cultural value system, national heritage, inculcation of scientific temper, observance of small family norms, secularism, democracy and socialism. The National system of education envisages a common educational structure of 10+2+3 which has been already accepted in all part of the country.

National Literacy Mission

To promote equality it will be necessary to provide for equal opportunity to all not only in access, but also in the condition for success. Adequate provisions have been made in the policy for education of SC/ST minorities. Handicapped and other educationally backward sections and areas.

Highest Priority

The New Education Policy, however gives the highest priority to solving the problems of children dropping out school and will adopt an array of meticulously formulated strategies based on micro planning, and applied at the grass roots level all over the country, to ensure children's retention at school.

Operation Blackboard

It is the endeavour in the New Education Policy to provide minimum essential facilities in primary, schools *viz.*, two reasonably large rooms that can be used in all weathers, the necessary toys, equipment, maps, charts, other learning material including the blackboard. An 'Operation Blackboard is being undertaken throughout the country as a part of the school improvement programme. It symbolises doing things at the right time, the right sprit and the right way by the right people. It is a programme of providing minimum essential facilities to all the primary schools in the country.

Women's Education

Education will be used as an agent of basic change in the status of women and women's empowerment. A component of women's development is being added to all the on-going programmes of the Department. For example:

(*a*) Stress on women teachers, while providing an additional teachers under operation blackboard.

(*b*) Non-formal Education to be treated as a programme of courses and special training of women instructors.

(*c*) National Literacy Mission to have a special focus on women's equality and running of centres for women.

(*d*) In vocationalisation, programmes for women's vocationalisation have been given special stress.

(*e*) A large programme of women's polytechnic *i.e.*, being taken up in technical education.

(*f*) Women's studies would continue to receive attention in higher education.

Navodaya Schools

The New Education policy fully takes care of providing open avenues of quality education to the masses. This was the concept behind the proposal to establish model schools now called Navodaya schools in every districts in the country. These schools are meant for the talented children of poor living in rural, tribal and hilly areas. The major thrust of these Navodaya Vidyalaya's is to promote national integration by taking the children from one part of the country to another and put them together so that they grow up another as Indians braking the traditional, social, regional and economic barriers. On the contrary, the new vidyalayas will be pace setting institution with full scope for innovation and experimentation which will cater to the creative expression and ability of the rural poor children.

Vocationalisation

Vocationalisation has received a very high priority in the new policy. It is envisaged that the point council of vocational education will be an umbrella body under the ministry of Human Resource Development which will also incorporate representation from all existing vocational education/training authorities and state government.

Open University

The New Education policy also provides for rural university which will be developed on the lines of Mahatma Gandhi's revolutionary ideas on education for the transformation of rural areas.

The first open university in India was established on 20th August, 1982 at Hyderabad and was inaugurated by the president of India. The open university is a direct outcome of the failure of the formal system of education to deliver the goods.

Examination Reforms

The New Education policy lays special emphasis on evaluation process and examination reforms. It lays down that assessment of performance is n integral part of any process of learning and teaching. As part of second educational strategy examination should be employed to bring about qualitative improvement in education.

National Policy of Education – 1986

The National Policy of Education 1986 marks a significant step in the history of education in free India. It was initiated by the Government of India to enable the country to promote its socio-cultural identity and to equip the country to face the challenges of the twenty first century. In 1985, the Government published 'The Challenge in Education' an important document containing guidelines for the future policy of education in India. After detailed debates and discussions at various levels, the national policy of education was formulated and it was passed by the Parliament in 1986.

The national policy of education is formulated on the basis of the directive principles and values enshrined in the constitution of India. The cultural and spiritual tradition of India, democratization, national integration and modernisation are seriously discussed in this policy.

The National system of education, Navodaya Schools, Vocational targets, de-linking degrees from jobs, performances and accountability, Indian educational service etc., are some of the admirable innovations in the new education policy.

Tangible results have been obtained in Operation, Black Board, Navodaya schools, mass-orientation of teachers and computer training and literacy mission.

REFERENCES

1. *Constitution of India* – by C. K. Jain.
2. *Constitution Amendment in India* – by Dr. R. C. Bhardwaj
3. *School Education in 1990's* – NCERT Publication.
4. *Teacher and Education in Indian Society* – by Dr. K. V. Eapen.
5. Ismail Thamarasseri (2008), *Early Childhood and Elementary Education*. New Delhi: Kanishka Publishers.

6

Education for Secularism and Secularisation of Education

The meaning of secularism different to country to country. European secularism emerge as a protest against Christianity in 19th century. The meaning of secularism different in India and Europe. Webster says, "Secularism, a system of doctrines and practices that rejects any form of religious faith and worship". Gandhiji says, "We believe in Sarva Dharma Samabhavana having equal regard for all faith and greeds". Dr. B. R. Ambedkar explains, "Secular state doesn't mean that it shall not take in to consideration the religious sentiments of the people. All that secular state means is that this parliament shall not be competent to impose any particular religion upon the rest of the people. This is the only limitation that the constitution recognises (*Parliamentary Debates, 1951, Vol III*, Part II). Thiserm secularism incorporated in the constitution by 42nd constitutional amendment in 1976. But the constitutional frame workers have a clear cut idea regarding since constitution framing. We are not following western concept of secularism fully, we indianise it. Secularism is an attitude and belief. It is not antireligious or irreligious. It doesn't rejecting any religion.

The Characteristics of a Secular Sate/Secularism as State's Policy

- The state as such has no religion of its own.
- It doesn't accord preferential treatment to the followers or any faith.
- It doesn't discriminate against any person on account of his faith.
- All citizens are eligible to enter government service irrespective of their faith.
- Consider religion as personal issues.
- State not support any religion and not controlled by any religion.

Educational Implications of Secularism

In a multi religious country like India, the spirit of secularism is to be developed in order to maintain the unity and integrity of the nation. Education should play a positive role in preparing people for a secular society and a purposeful life. We hope secularism will develop in to stronger force leading to the social unity of India. When institutionalised religions gradually lose their co-ersive hold on the younger generation. A process in which the dominance of religion over other institutions is reduced, is called secularisation. According to Brubacher secularism has "no religious point of view while it has a theory of moral education". Brubacher has also observed, "if the secularist has any religion at all it is likely that scientific doctrine constitutes the presuppositions of that religion and that scientists are its high priests". Secularism is a philosophy of moral education. Secular behaviour springs in the school from the influence of the school, through the conduct and behaviours of the teachers themselves and little in the school community as a whole. All the activities and programmes of the schools must strive for the inculcation of values of love, truth and tolerance.

Indian Constitution and Secularism

- *Article 19(1)*: "Subject to public order, morality and health and to other provisions of this part, all personas are equally entitled to freedom to conscience and the right freely to profess, practise and propagate religion".

- *Article 21*: "No person may be compelled to pay any taxes, the proceeds of which are specifically appropriated in payment of expenses for the promotion or maintenance of any particular religion or religious denomination".
- *Article 22(1)*: "No religious instruction shall be provided in any educational institution wholly maintained out of state funds". Provided that nothing in this clause shall apply to an education institution which is administered but has been established under an endowment or trust which requires that religious instructions shall be imparted in such institutions.
- *Article 22(2)*: No person attending any educational institution recognised by the state of receiving aid out of state funds shall be required to take part in any religious institution or to attend any religious worship that may be conducted in such institution or in any premises attached there to unless such person, or if such person is a minor his guardian has given his consent thereto".
- *Article 30(1)*: "All minorities whether based on religion or language, shall have the right to establish and administer educational institutions of their choice".
- *Article 30(2)*: "The state shall not in granting aid to educational institutions, discriminate against any educational institution of the ground that it is under the management of minority, whether based on religion or language".

The Education Commission (1964-66) on Religious Education and Education About Religion

"We suggest that a syllabus giving all chosen information about each of the major religions should be included as a part of the course in citizenship or as a part of general education to be introduced in schools and colleges upto the first degree. It should be highlight the fundamental similarities in the great religions of the world and the emphasis they place the cultivation of certain broadly comparable moral and spiritual values".

Secularism in India

India is a secular country as per the declaration in the Preamble to the indian constitution. It prohibits discrimination against members of a particular religion, race, caste, sex or place of birth. The Indian notion for the term secularism is different from the French notion for the term. The word secular was inserted into the preamble by the 42nd Amendment. (1976) It implies equality of all religions and religious tolerance and respect. India, therefore does not have an official state religion. Every person has the right to preach, practice and propagate any religion they choose. The government must not favour or discriminate against any religion. It must treat all religions with equal respect. All citizens, irrespective of their religious beliefs are equal in front of law. No religious instruction is imparted in government or government-aided schools. Nevertheless, general information about all established world religions is imparted as part of the course in Sociology, without giving any importance to any one religion or the others. The content presents the basic/ fundamental information with regards to the fundamental beliefs, social values and main practices and festivals of each established world religions. The Supreme Court in *S. R. Bommai v. Union of India* held that secularism was an integral part of the basic structure of the constitution.

History of Secularism

Religions of India are known to have co-existed and evolved together for many centuries predating Republic of India. Indian civilization is among the oldest and living civilizations of the modern world. India is a country where religion is very central to the life of many people. India's age-old philosophy as expounded in Hindu scriptures called Upanishads is *sarva dharma samabhava,* which means respect for all belief systems. This basic trait of *Sanatan dharma* is what keeps India together despite the fact that India has not been a mono-religious country for over two millennium. A Hindu Nationalist school of thought also proclaims that with Sanatan Dharma being the spirit of India, the very concept of western secularism is redundant and badly imposed. Some researchers believe that the history of Indian secularism begin with the protest movements in the 5th century BC. The three main protest movements were by the Charvakas (a secularistic and materialistic philosophical movement), Buddhism, and Jainism. All three of them rejected the authority of the Vedas and any importance of belief in a deity.

Secularism in British India

In the 18th century, when the British East India Company began to gain total control over India that ideas of secularism began to impact on the Indian mind. Until then, religion was considered to be inseparable from political and social life. The British codified laws pertaining to practices within religions on the sub-continents. This began when the Governor of Calcutta Warren Hastings set out his Judicial Plan in 1772 and 1774, this was a judicial system that codified civil, criminal and commercial laws, while family law and some property laws were still governed by Muslim and Hindu religious law, not to mention religious laws of Christians, Sikhs, Parsis and other faiths. Some see this as a part of their divide-and-rule policy. In doing so they laid the foundation for a non-uniform civil code which remains largely unchanged to date. This is a major grouse for Hindu politicians who insist that there should be a uniform civil code for all citizens. For example, believers of all faiths other than Islam are legally bound to be monogamous while those who practice or convert to Islam are permitted up to four marriages, which is therefore not uniform behaviour. In India, right from the British period, main contradiction was not between religious and secular but it was between secular and communal. In the western world main struggle was between church and state and church and civil society but in India neither Hinduism nor Islam had any church-like structure and hence there never was any such struggle between secular and religious power structure. The main struggle was between secularism and communalism. The communal forces from among Hindus and Muslims mainly fought for share in power though they used their respective religions for their struggle for power.

Secularism in Modern India

Buddhist monks at the Sera Monastery during a festival. The monastery was granted asylum by the India and relocated to Mysore after the Chinese invasion of Tibet. After independence and partition, a large body of Muslims were left in India and hence leaders like Gandhi and Nehru preferred to keep India secular in the sense that the Republic of India shall have no national religion and the people of India shall be free both in any individual and corporate sense to follow any religion of their choice. Thus India remained politically secular and its people continued to passionately practise their religions.

Jawaharlal Nehru, the first Prime Minister of India, was a supporter of secularism and secular politics. Theoretically speaking the Congress Party was also committed to secularism. However, the Congress Party consisted of several members and leaders whose secular political principles are doubtable. But it was due to Mahatma Gandhi, Nehru, Maulana Abul Kalam Azad and B. R. Ambedkar that India committed itself to secularism and its Constitution was drafted on secular lines. Secularism in India, as pointed out before, emphasised upon the principles of equal respect for all religions and cultures and non-interference of religion in the government affairs. Also, according to the Indian Constitution no discrimination shall be made on the basis of caste, creed, gender and class. Similarly all citizens of India irrespective of one's religion, caste or gender have right to vote. According to articles 14 to 21 all will enjoy same rights without any discrimination on any ground. According to Article 25 all those who reside in India are free to confess, practice and propagate religion of one's choice subject of course to social health and law and order. Thus even conversion to any religion of ones choice is a fundamental right. In fact, in India an overwhelming majority of people are religious but are tolerant and respect other religions and are thus 'secular' in the Indian context. Even Sufis and Bhakti Saints are considered quite secular in that sense. The word secularism has had multiple interpretations, namely: an agnostic interpretation and a pluralistic interpretation. While Nehru, Mohammed Ali Jinnah, and Subhas Chandra Bose subscribed to the agnostic interpretation of Secularism, Gandhiji and others believed in pluralistic interpretation of Secularism.

The Preamble to the Constitution of India grants "liberty of thought, expression, belief, faith and worship" immediately after proclaiming that India is a 'Sovereign Socialist Secular Democratic Republic'. This reading of the constitution suggests that the Constitution of India has a pluralistic interpretation of Secularism. Also, religious belief governs the application of laws in India (Indian law), which indicates a pluralistic interpretation of the term Secularism in the Indian legal system. The science of the concept of legal pluralism and the study of legal pluralism as it has naturally existed in India is on-going. There are some atheists and secularists who reject religion in its entirety but such people are extremely few. Though there are no census figures available but one can safely say that there are less than 0.1 per cent in India. Also, there are extremely orthodox people who exhibit rigidity and intolerance towards other faiths though of course not on communal grounds but on the grounds of religious orthodoxy but they too are in minuscule minority. Tolerance in India among people of all religions is widely prevalent. It is perhaps due to influence of ancient Vedic doctrine that truth is one but is manifested in different forms. Thus the real spirit of secularism in India is all-inclusiveness, religious pluralism and peaceful co-existence. However, it is politics, which proved to be divisive and not religion. It is not religious leaders by and large (with few exceptions) who divide but politicians who seek to mobilise votes on grounds of divisive identities like religion, caste and ethnicity. In a multi-religious society, if politics is not based on issues but on identities, it can prove highly divisive. Politicians are tempted to appeal to such identities rather than to solve problems. The former case proves much easier. The medieval society in India was thus more religiously tolerant as it was non-competitive. The modern Indian society, on the other hand, has proved to be more divisive as it is based on competition.

REFERENCES

1. Ismail Thamarasseri (2007), *Education in the Emerging Indian Society*. New Delhi: Kanishka Publishers.
2. http://en.wikipedia.org/wiki/Secularism_in_India

7 Democracy and Education

Democracy

Is a form of government in which all eligible citizens participate equally – either directly or through elected representatives – in the proposal, development, and creation of laws. It encompasses social, economic and cultural conditions that enable the free and equal practice of political self-determination. Abraham Lincoln defined, "Democracy as the government of the people, by the people and for the people. But, based on our present experiences – communal riots, politrics, red-tapism, corruption – we can change that definition to "Democracy as the government off the people, buy the people and fore/foray the people".

The word democracy derived from:

Demo = people

Kratia = power

Democracy has two aspects:

1. Democracy as a way of life (*John Stuart Mill*). That is, an attitude or life style from the angle of people.
2. Democracy as a machinery, from the view of ruling class/ government. In this dimension includes a 'power/control'.

In a comprehensive outlook, democracy is the emancipation of man's liberation from all social bondages, like poverty, etc. The basic principles of democracy are, justice, liberty, equality and fraternity. William Kornblum defines, democracy "A political system in which all citizens have the right to participate in public decision-making" (*William Kornblum, Sociology – The central questions*).

Education and Democracy

Democracy, we know it's a philosophy of modern life style and education is a tool to achieve modernisation and social change. Therefore there two must be highly connected. Prof. Dewey in his book 'Democracy and Education' has explained the relationship in these words, "an undesirable society is one which internally and externally sets up barriers to free inter course and communication of experience. A society which makes provisions for participation in its good of all its members on equal terms and which secures flexible re-adjustment of its institutions through the interaction of the different forms of associated life is so far democratic, such a society must have a type of education which gives individuals a personal interest in social relationships and control and the habits of mind which secure social changes without introducing disorder".

'Preparing students to democracy' are of the aim of education. For strengthening Indian democracy we must give importance to some aims of education for the same. The Secondary Education Commission (1952-53) has suggested the following aims of education of a democratic society.

1. Development of democratic citizenship.
2. Improvement of vocational efficiency.
3. Development of personality.
4. Development of qualities of leadership.

Education for democracy doesn't mean just providing of some facts on democracy but must acquire attitudes, interests, skills to assimilate that philosophy. Education for democracy is a kind of citizenship training. Who is a citizen?

Any one born as a citizen? What is the difference between a citizen and an individual? Citizen was not born but made. How? 'Education!', the only answer. We can train students for better students in school society. It prepares them to a citizen. He must aware about the fundamental duties and rights. Right implies duties. But now-a-days educated fellows even think about how save/escape from income tax? In our beloved country there is no progress in social and economic democracy. But only political democracy we experience.

The theoretical study of rights and duties not made any effect in society. But we need the formation of democracy as a life style. For that our schools atmosphere must be democratic. Our nation, land of diversities, leads to issues problems. But everything can be solved through education for democracy.

Educational Implications

Democracy is the result of education. Unless the principles of democracy are reflected in the aims and ideals of education, curriculum, methods of teaching, administration and organization, in discipline, in the atmosphere of the school and in the outlook of the teacher, democracy cannot grow. If democracy can catch roots anywhere, it is in the school, which is a very rich and fertile field for its growth and development.

Democratic Aims

The first goal in education in and for democracy is the full rounded and continuing development of the person.

Education in democracy must create democratic personality it must discover his potentialities and then enable him to realise them to the full by utilising the facilities provided to the individuals. It must equip the individual with the power of judgement, scientific thinking and weighing the right and the wrong. The individual must be made aware of the ideals of life and he must grow in their context. Education must impart him correct knowledge of the political, social, religious and economic problems not only of his country but also of other countries. It must inculcate in his the spirit of tolerance for the views and modes of life of others and create in him a passion for social justice which should help him to have board and spirit of service. The individual's personality must have emotional balance. He must be mentally healthy, accept in himself, accept others and behave in a manner that he should be accepted by others.

Democratic aim in education does not mean passing the examination or gathering knowledge only but to enable the individual to have intellectual and moral qualities which must change his outlook.

Democratic Curriculum

Pragmatists say that children should learn what they are interested in this is an erroneous view. In fact, the children should be made interested to know what they need to know, though it is not always possible to interest all the children all the time in every thing they need to know. But teachers, however, use motivation to interest the child in knowing what he should know.

Democratic curriculum should have variety and flexibility so as to be based upon the tastes and talents of children. The present higher secondary scheme is the vindication of this principle. Upto the 8th or 9th, the children are required to study a core curriculum or a knowledge which is essential and is fundamental for everyone to study irrespective of the role that he is to play in adult life.

Democratic curriculum is not subject curriculum alone. It includes every influence, every activity and every experience, which is educative. It is the total life and programme of the school, whether in classroom, in library or laboratory or in the play-field.

Democratic Methods and Techniques

New methods of instructions will produce citizens capable of accepting his challenges of the present and the future. Democrative teaching means a co-operative enterprise. Teaching, planning and execution of subject lessons and other educative activities are done by the pupils and the teachers together. It does not believe in the domination of the teacher or the textbook. Just stuffing information into the child is undemocratic and the negation of psychology. The teacher should not impose anything. He should-encourage free enquiry and discussion. He should act as a guide, supervisor and inspirer. Group work, discussion, problem solving, learning through experiences and group evaluation of results are the chief characteristics of democratic methods. Stress is on intelligence, learning, thinking and subjects of enquiry. It is in this sense that the new education advocates Dalton plan, Montessori system, Heuristic methods, socialised recitation etc., as methods which aim at purposeful study.

It is true that the school is a formal institution, but the methods of teaching should be most natural and informal. In the words of Home "In the school the children should live and learn adequately, fully, richly, naturally, informally and creatively".

Democratic Administration and Organization

It is autocratic administration when the administrator thinks that he can sit by himself and see all angles of a problem. On the other hand, the democratic administrator realises the potential powers of other brains and knows how to use them.

In a democratically administered school the students have the share in making the rules which relate to them. They have ample opportunities to shoulder responsibilities in running clubs, societies and associations and in organizing various functions in the school. Activities like organizing games, running the school store or school canteen, looking after the cleanliness of the school, bringing out a school journal, magazine or news bulletin should be left over to the managements of students. While the guidance and advice of teachers should be available, the students must enjoy powers to take their own decisions and show a sense of responsibility.

Democratic education must be well planned, where in all the members work effectively, economically and harmoniously together to achieve a common purpose, where freedom is associated with responsibility. Democracy through co-curricular activities.

Co-curricular activities offer the pupils the best opportunity to manifest their self-reliance, qualities of leadership, initiative, co-operation, intelligent behaviour and responsible behaviour. They are the richest ground for the inculcation of democratic principles. One can learn to co-operate only by co-operating, to select leaders only by selecting leaders, to plan only by planning. In short, one can learn to live democratically only by living democratically.

Democratic Discipline

School is a laboratory in which children learn the arts and skills of democratic social living. Responsible co-operation and self discipline or free-discipline should be two key notes of such a laboratory. Self-discipline develop through firm but kind discipline from others. In training our students for democracy, we should stimulate in them not-only willing subordination to the constituted authority, but also such desirable qualities as intellectual honesty, fearless reasoning and respect for order based on inner conviction and willing acquiescence. Love, sympathy, human relationship should be the bonds between the teacher and the taught. Sit still keep quiet and do as you are told. These commandments tend to create a grave-yard discipline. There is no inner urge for obeying the laws and regulations of the school.

Discipline in democratic education is based on the conviction of doing the right thing in the right manner and at the right moment. It is based upon proper understanding of the nature of human relationships. Wherever there is provision for self development, there emerges an inner urge to obey the laws and regulations of the community.

Teacher in Democratic Education

A teacher in democracy should himself have adequate conceptual frame work of democracy. If he wants to increase pupil's understanding in this area. To clarify the pupil's understanding the teacher should have proficiency in using such classroom management and teaching techniques as pupil-teacher planning, group work, discussions and problem solving. (Besides giving children love and affection, the teacher must help to make them feel that they are important). Democracy and good citizenship come not from a course of studies but from a teacher, not from a curriculum but from a human soul.

The pre requisite of a democratic teacher is that he should recognise that environment is more important than heredity, that every individual is different from every other individual, that everyone is capable of making moral choices, of deciding what is true and false, good or bad, beautiful or ugly, that every child has a right to freedom, to think, to choose and equality of chances.

Democratic Atmosphere

It is the democratic environment which is congenial for the full flowering of human personality. Suppression and repression stifle the growth. An educational institution should be liberal and liberating institution. Equality of treatment should be the pervasive role. No pupil should be treated with Sarcasm or contempt. Snobbishness and selfishness should be discouraged. Everyone should know the efforts bring success and not the extraneous considerations. The atmosphere of strict adherence to tradition and blind loyalty will stop new ideas being tried and aired. The emphasis should be on constructive thinking. The headmaster should not turn a discouraging face on the teacher with a bright suggestion. Similarly the teacher should not pass off lightly what students have suggested. The head and staff should have profound respect for every one.

Democratisation of Education in India

The Acharya Narendra Dev Committee in 1938, the Muthaliar Commission in 1952 and the Kothari Commission in 1966 have suggested a large number of measures for democritising education at various levels, the progress in the direction has not yet been satisfactory. K. G. Saiyidain said, "In India, the forms and institutions of political democracy have been established, but the spirit which gives them reality and meaning has yet to grow, for this purpose education should devote itself to the cultivation of the attitudes and ideals which are needed for the successful implementation of democracy.

The phenomenal expansion at all stages of education especially school education with the increase in the number of schools, teachers, pupils and expenditure therein, a large number of measures for improving the economic and social status of teachers, provision of multifarious incentives and facilities for the weaker and deprived sections of the community like free supply of textbooks and writing materials, free school uniforms, attendance scholarships, construction of quarters in tribal areas, establishment of Textbook Banks etc., can undoubtedly be treated as clear indications of the landslide drift in the direction of democratisation. The institution of various merit scholarships and loan scholarships provide educational opportunities to the deprived.

We have so far been trying to equalise educational opportunities through three main prorgrammes *(a)* expansion of faculties at all stages *(b)* provision of free-education *(c)* maintenance of low fees in higher education. These are the basic tools for the equalisation of educational opportunities and this is the basic tenet in democratic education.

When functional democracy is established in the entire educational system, structure and institutions, democritisation is not only possible but also be stabilised.

Aspects of Democracy

(i) Political Democracy

Democracy is founded upon the principle of popular sovereignty *i.e.,* ultimate power resides in the citizens. An important principle of democracy is that all citizens have equal political privileges which only they can exercise and which they cannot transfer to any other persons. Another foundational principle is that rule of the majority shall prevail, this majority to be expressed by the citizens through direct voting or through their elected representatives. A third principle is that citizens can vote the government out of office.

Political democracy is that in which every adult has the right to govern the country. The rule does not lie "Into the hands of a small body of men or even into the hands of one class in the community". According to Dicey, "Democracy is a form of government in which governing body is comparatively larger fraction of the entire nation".

(ii) Economic Democracy

This is the second important aspects of democracy. Economic democracy means a democracy in which the economic resources or means are not monopolised by a few capitalists but economic power is in the hands of majority. Every individual will provided work according to his abilities and capabilities. This aspect of democracy is found only in a socialist country. There labour is honoured and given the best possible facilities. In India, we have achieved political freedom. No doubt, but economic freedom is still to be achieved and this can only be possible through increased production and economic democracy.

In a democracy, economic and social equality must flourish, "without economic equality and equal opportunities, human energies are bound to be go waste and to rot; individual development and social progress are bound to be impossibilities with destruction and violence into the bargain".

(iii) Social Democracy

This aspects of democracy indicates "all distinctions based on class, birth or possession of money"– must be done away with. There must not be any problem of caste and creed. Every man is born equal and has the equal status in the society.

Importance of Education in Democracy

1. *Education for Citizenship:* The educational system must make its contribution to the development of habits, attitudes and qualities of character, which will enable the citizens to bear worthily the responsibilities of democratic citizenship and to counteract all those

tendencies which hinder the emergence of a broad, national and secular outlook.

2. *Education for Improving Productive Efficiency:* One of its most urgent problems is to improve productive efficiency to increase the national wealth and thereby to raise the standard of living.
3. *Stimulating of Cultural Renaissance:* As a result of the oppressive and widespread poverty, there is a serious lack of educational facilities and the bulk of the people are so obsessed with the problem of some sort of living that they have not been to give sufficient attention to cultural pursuits.

Views of Secondary Education Commission (1952)

The commission discovered defects which were at the root of the prevailing system. The defects are as follows:

1. Education was too bookish and Mechanical, stereotypical and rigidly uniform and did not cater to the different aptitudes of the pupil.
2. The existing system did not develop the basic qualities of discipline, co-operation and leadership.
3. The stress on examinations, the over-crowded syllabus, the method of teaching an the lack of proper material amenities tended to make education a burden rather than a joyous experience to the youthful mind.
4. Rigid time-table, unsuitable textbooks, and unduly detailed syllabus.
5. Due to heavy strength, the classes suffer from the proper attention and guidance by the teacher.
6. The existing secondary education is isolated from life. After the youths come out of their school, they feel ill-adjusted. Their whole personality is not trained – their practical aptitudes, emotions, sense of appreciation and tasks are largely ignored.

Secondary Education Commission recommended that Secondary Education should aim at developing the following qualities in the future citizens.

(i) ***Intellectual, Social and Moral Qualities***

- To live with others and to appreciate the value of co-operation.
- He should have social awakening.
- Thinking and reasoning capacities should be cultivated.
- Ability to carry on one's burden.
- Ability and desire for social upliftment.
- The understanding an the intellectual integrity to shift truth from falsehood, facts from propaganda and to reject the dangerous appeal of fanaticism and prejudice.

(ii) ***Vocational Ability***

- The pupils should be encouraged to acquire a yearning for the perfection and learn to take in doing everything.
- Craft education should be encouraged.
- Diversification of courses should be introduced.

(iii) ***To Create Means for a Harmonious Development of the Personality***

- The children should be enabled to develop psychologically, socially and emotionally in accordance with their practical needs.
- The commission prescribed for the appreciation of the cultural-heritage and subjects like art, craft, and music.
- Hobbies should be developed.

Recommendation of Education Commission

The Education Commission (1966) under the leadership of Dr. D. S. Kothari submitted some important suggestions.

1. Re-organize our educational pattern, change our syllabi to improve our examination system.
2. Major improvement in the effectiveness of primary education.

3. Work experience as an integral element of general education.
4. Vocationalise secondary education.
5. Improve the quality of teachers at all levels and to provide teachers in sufficient strength.
6. Strengthen centres of advanced study and strive to attain, in some our universities at least, higher international standards; to lay special emphasis on the combination of teaching and research.
7. Pay particular attention to education and research in agriculture and allied sciences.

Functions of the School in a Democracy

1. To convey to the students the meaning of democratic values, ideals and principles and their implications for conduct in the various life situations.
2. To enable the students to incorporate these values, ideas and principles in their daily conduct, in and out of school.
3. A democratic school introduces radical changes in respects of methods, discipline and administration.

Methods of Educating the Students in a Democratic Way of Life

- Respect of individual personality.
- Introduction of self-government in schools.
- Provision for manual work.
- Equal opportunities for admission.
- Encouragement to group work.
- Democratic methods of teaching.
- Promotion of self-expression.
- Opportunities for social service.
- Vocational efficiency.
- Development of hobbies.
- Hostel life.
- Student parliament.
- Visits to legislature.

REFERENCE

1. Ismail Thamarasseri (2007), *Education in the Emerging Indian Society*. New Delhi: Kanishka Publishers.
2. http://en.wikipedia.org/wiki/DEMOCRACY

8 Values Laid Down in the Constitution of India

Sovereignty

To uphold and Protest the Sovereignty, Unity and Integrity of India is one of fundamental duty of Indian Citizens. In a democratic system of governance, sovereignty lies with the people. To defend our sovereignty is our own responsibility. If the freedom and unity of the country are jeopardized, the nation ceases to exist and if there is no nation, who lives?

Sovereignty is the quality of having independent authority over a geographic area, such as a territory. It can be found in a power to rule and make laws that rests on a political fact for which no pure legal definition can be provided. In theoretical terms, the idea of 'sovereignty', historically, from Socrates to Thomas Hobbes, has always necessitated a moral imperative on the entity exercising it. For centuries past, the idea that a state could be sovereign was always connected to its ability to guarantee the best interests of its own citizens. Thus, if a state could not act in the best interests of its own citizens, it could not be thought of as a 'sovereign' state. The concept of sovereignty has been discussed throughout history, from the time of the Romans through to the present day. It has changed in its definition, concept, and application throughout, especially during the Age of Enlightenment. The current notion of state sovereignty contains four aspects consisting of territory, population, authority and recognition. According to Stephen D. Krasner, the term could also be understood in four different ways:

1. *Domestic Sovereignty*: Actual control over a state exercised by an authority organized within this state.
2. *Interdependence Sovereignty*: Actual control of movement across state's borders, assuming the borders exist.
3. *International Legal Sovereignty*: Formal recognition by other sovereign states.
4. *Westphalian Sovereignty*: Lack of other authority over state than the domestic authority (examples of such other authorities could be a non-domestic church, a non-domestic political organization, or any other external agent).

Often, these four aspects all appear together, but this is not necessarily the case – they are not affected by one another, and there are historical examples of states that were non-sovereign in one aspect while at the same time being sovereign in another of these aspects. According to Immanuel Wallerstein, another fundamental feature of sovereignty is that its a claim that must be recognised by others if there is to have any meaning: "Sovereignty is more than anything else a matter of legitimacy [...that] requires reciprocal recognition. Sovereignty is a hypothetical trade, in which two potentially conflicting sides, respecting de facto realities of power, exchange such recognitions as their least costly strategy.

Socialism

As an economic and political philosophy, socialism began as an attack on the concepts of private property and personal profit. These aspects of capitalism, socialists believed, should be replaced by public ownership of property and sharing profits.

Robert Owen in England, Henri de Saint Simon (France) and in 19th century Karl Marx (USSR) is the proponents of socialism. Karl Marx observed, socialist state must be controlled by working class.

Definition

"An economic philosophy based on the concept of public ownership of property and sharing of profits, together with the belief that economic decision should be controlled by the workers". – William Kornblum, 1998.

Meaning

Socialism has its origin in Europe as a revolt against capitalism in the 19th century. Its salient ideas spread all over the world. These are different brands/forms or socialism especially those shared by Karl Marx Lenin in Russia, Mao in China and Gandhi in India. In 1947 in an editorial under the caption 'who is a socialist' Gandhi wrote, "under socialism all the members of the society are equal-none low, none high ..... Even as members or the individual body are equal, so are the members of the society. This is socialism, under it, the prince and the peasant, the wealthy and the poor, the employer and the employee are all on the same level".

Socialism is a scheme of social organization, which places the means of production and distribution in the hands of the community. Socialism is part and parcel of the concept of the welfare state. By planning and fully utilising all the resources available in the country, it seeks to provide maximum benefit to all the people".

Characteristics/Features

- Socialism aims at social justice.
- It aims at equality.
- It aims a class less society, free from exploitation, oppression and disparity.
- It pre-supposes public ownership of the means of production.
- It aims at active participation of the individual in the productive process of society.

- It aims at establishing a society based on mental co-operation and fellow feeling.
- It aims at abolishing the capitalist system.
- It aims at developing necessary skills and favourable attitudes towards work.

Indian Constitution and Socialism

Through the 42nd constitutional amendment on 1976 the term socialism included in our constitution. Unto that it implicit in 4th chapter, directive principles of state policy. Based on the implicit/hidden one our parliament accept the idea of 'socialistic pattern of society' in 1954. In economy we stand between capitalism and socialism *i.e.*, mixed economy. We aim a democratic socialist nation. We keep both socialist ideals and basic human rights.

Educational Implications of Socialism

Aims of Education and Socialism, Emphasis on

- Social development of an individual.
- Education for citizenship.
- Socialisation of the individual.

Contents/Curriculum

- More emphasis on core curriculum.
- Subject matter stressing equality.
- Study of socialistic movements.
- Socially useful productive work and work experience.

Methods of Teaching

- Socialised recitation techniques.
- Project method.
- Problem method.
- Team teaching.

Educational Measures for Promoting a Socialist Society

Kothari commission observed, "one of the important social objectives of education is to equalise opportunity, enabling the backward or under privileged classes and individuals to use education as a lever for the improvement of their condition. Every society that values social justice and is anxious to improve the lot of the common man and cultivate all available talent, must ensure progressive equality of opportunity to all section of population. This is the only guarantee for the building up of an egalitarian and human society in which the exploitation of the weak will be minimized".

Teaching of Socialism

It is the responsibility of the educational institutions to bring about adequate awareness regarding socialism among the teachers and students so that the young people are armed with knowledge which will enable them to chart the course of the nation towards the goal of socialism. The following are three main ways in which a school can convey positive attitudes and values regarding socialism to students:

- Direct teaching of socialism.
- Living the values and attitudes to be learned through the organization of various activities.
- Teachers becoming models embodying the desired values and attitudes.

Text Books and Socialism

As an impact of socialism, text-books at the school stage, by and large, have been nationalized. The contents of text-books are oriented and regulated according to the national policy and ethos. Efforts are being made to keep the price range of text books within the easy reach of the parents.

Secularism

The meaning of secularism different to country to country. European secularism emerge as a protest against Christianity in 19th century. The meaning of secularism different in India and Europe. Webster says, "Secularism, a system of doctrines and practices that rejects any form of religious faith and worship". Gandhiji says, "We believe in Sarva Dharma Samabhavana having equal regard for all faith and greeds".

Dr. B. R. Ambedkar explains, "Secular state doesn't mean that it shall not take in to consideration the religious sentiments of the people. All that secular state means is that this parliament shall not be competent to impose any particular religion upon the rest of the people. This is the only limitation that the constitution recognises (*Parliamentary Debates, 1951, Vol-III*, Part II).

This term secularism incorporated in the constitution by 42nd constitutional amendment in 1976. But the constitutional frame workers have a clear cut idea regarding since constitution framing. We are not following western concept of secularism fully, we indianise it. Secularism is an attitude and belief. It is not antireligious or irreligious. It doesn't rejecting any religion.

The Characteristics of a Secular Sate/Secularism as State's Policy

- The state as such has no religion of its own.
- It doesn't accord preferential treatment to the followers or any faith.
- It doesn't discriminate against any person on account of his faith.
- All citizens are eligible to enter government service irrespective of their faith.
- Consider religion as personal issues.
- State not support any religion and not controlled by any religion.

Educational Implications of Secularism

In a multi religious country like India, the spirit of secularism is to be developed in order to maintain the unity and integrity of the nation. Education should play a positive role in preparing people for a secular society and a purposeful life. Secularism will develop in to stronger force leading to the social unity of India. A process, in which the dominance of religion over other institutions is reduced, is called secularisation.

According to Brubacher secularism has "no religious point of view while it has a theory of moral education". Brubacher has also observed, "If the secularist has any religion at all it is likely that scientific doctrine constitutes the presuppositions of that religion and that scientists are its high priests".

Secularism is a philosophy of moral education. Secular behaviour springs in the school from the influence of the school, through the conduct and behaviours of the teachers themselves and little in the school community as a whole. All the activities and programmes of the schools must strive for the inculcation of values of love, truth and tolerance.

Religions and Moral Education in Secular India/Indian Constitution and Secularism

- *Article 19(1)*: "Subject to public order, morality and health and to other provisions of this part, all personas are equally entitled to freedom to conscience and the right freely to profess, practise and propagate religion".
- *Article 21*: "No person may be compelled to pay any taxes, the proceeds of which are specifically appropriated in payment of expenses for the promotion or maintenance of any particular religion or religious denomination".
- *Article 22(1)*: "No religious instruction shall be provided in any educational institution wholly maintained out of state funds".

Provided that nothing in this clause shall apply to an education institution which is administered but has been established under an endowment or trust which requires that religious instructions shall be imparted in such institutions.

- *Article 22(2)*: No person attending any educational institution recognised by the state of receiving aid out of state funds shall be required to take part in any religious institution or to attend any religious worship that may be conducted in such institution or in any premises attached there to unless such person, or if such person is a minor his guardian has given his consent thereto".
- *Article 30(1)*: "All minorities whether based on religion or language, shall have the right to establish and administer educational institutions of their choice".
- *Article 30(2)*: "The state shall not in granting aid to educational institutions, discriminate against any

educational institution of the ground that it is under the management of minority, whether based on religion or language".

The Education Commission (1964-66) on Religious Education and Education About Religion

"We suggest that a syllabus giving all chosen information about each of the major religions should be included as a part of the course in citizenship or as a part of general education to be introduced in schools and colleges upto the first degree. It should be highlight the fundamental similarities in the great religions of the world and the emphasis they place the cultivation of certain broadly comparable moral and spiritual values".

Democracy

Abraham Lincoln defined, "Democracy as the government of the people, by the people and for the people. Democracy has two aspects, *i.e.*

In a comprehensive outlook, democracy is the emancipation of man's liberation from all social bondages, like poverty, etc. The basic principles of democracy are, justice, liberty, equality and fraternity. William Kornblum defines, democracy "A political system in which all citizens have the right to participate in public decision making" (*William Kornblum, Sociology – The central questions*).

Education and Democracy

Democracy, we know it's a philosophy of modern life style and education is a tool to achieve modernization and social change. Therefore there two must be highly connected. Prof. Dewey in his book 'Democracy and Education' has explained the relationship in these words, "an undesirable society is one which internally and externally sets up barriers to free inter course and communication of experience. A society which makes provisions for participation in its good of all its members on equal terms and which secures flexible re-adjustment of its institutions through the interaction of the different forms of associated life is so far democratic, such a society must have a type of education which gives individuals a personal interest in social relationships and control and the habits of mind which secure social changes without introducing disorder".

Education for Democracy

'Preparing students to democracy' are of the aim of education. For strengthening Indian democracy we must give importance to some aims of education for the same. The Secondary Education Commission (1952-53) has suggested the following aims of education of a democratic society.

- Development of democratic citizenship.
- Improvement of vocational efficiency.
- Development of personality.
- Development of qualities of leadership.

Republic

A republic is a country where power is held by the people or the representatives that they elect. Republic has presidents who are elected, rather than kings or queens. India is a republic. As opposed to a monarchy, in which the head of state is appointed on hereditary basis for a lifetime or until he abdicates from the throne, a democratic republic is an entity in which the head of state is elected, directly or indirectly, for a fixed tenure. The President of India is elected by an electoral college for a term of five years. The post of the President of India is not hereditary. Every citizen of India is eligible to become the President of the country. The leaders of the state and local bodies are also elected by the people in similar manner..

A republic is a form of government in which the country is considered a 'public matter' (Latin: *res publica*), not the private concern or property of the rulers, and where offices of state are subsequently directly or indirectly elected or appointed rather than inherited. In modern times, a common simplified definition of a republic is a government where the head of state is not a monarch. Currently, 135 of the world's 206 sovereign statesuse the word 'republic' as part of their official names.

Both modern and ancient republics vary widely in their ideology and composition. In classical and medieval times the archetype of all republics was the Roman Republic, which referred to Rome in between the period when it had kings, and the periods when it had emperors. The Italian medieval and Renaissance political tradition today referred to as 'civic humanism' is sometimes considered to derive directly from Roman republicans such as Sallust and Tacitus. However, Greek-influenced Roman authors, such as Polybius and Cicero, sometimes also used the term as a translation for the Greek *politeia* which could mean regime generally, but could also be applied to certain specific types of regime which did not exactly correspond to that of the Roman Republic. Republics were not equated with classical democracies such as Athens, but had a democratic aspect. In modern republics such as the United States, France, Russia, India, and Mexico the executiveis legitimized both by a constitution and by popular suffrage. Montesquieu included both democracies, where all the people have a share in rule, and aristocracies or oligarchies, where only some of the people rule, as republican forms of government.

Most often a republic is a sovereign state, but there are also sub-sovereign state entities that are referred to as republics, or which have governments that are described as 'republican' in nature. For instance, Article IV of the Constitution of the United States "guarantee(s) to every State in this Union a Republican form of Government". The subdivisions of the Soviet Union were described as republics and two of them – Ukrainian SSR and Byelorussian SSR – had their own seats at the United Nations. While the Constitution of the Soviet Union described that union as a 'unitary, federal and multinational state', it was in reality a unitary state since the Communist Party of the Soviet Union exercised a centralized form of authority over the nominally-autonomous Soviet Socialist Republics. In the early 20th century a number of Indian scholars, most notably as K. P. Jayaswal, argued that a number of states in ancient India had republican forms of government. There are no surviving constitutions or works of political philosophy from this period in Indian history. The forms of government thus need to be deduced, mostly from the surviving religious texts. These texts do refer to a number of states having *GaGasangha*, or council-based, as opposed to monarchical governments.

A second form of evidence comes from Greeks writing about India during the period of contact following the conquests of Alexander. Greek writers about India such as Megasthenes and Arrian describe many of the states having republican governments akin to those of Greece. Beginning around 700 BC, republics developed in a band running along the Indus Valley in the northwest and along the Ganges Plain in the northeast. They were mainly small states, though some confederations of republics seem to have formed that covered large areas, such as Vajjian Confederacy, which had Vaishali as its capital around 600 BC.

As in Greece, the republican era came to an end in the 4th century with the rise of a monarchical empire. The Maurya Empire conquered almost the entire subcontinent, ending the autonomy of the small republics. Some did remain republics under Mauryan suzerainty, or returned to being republics after the fall of the empire. Madra, for instance, survived as a republic until the 4th century AD. The final end of republics in India came with the rise of the Gupta Empire, and an associated philosophy of the divine nature of monarchy.

Justice

Indian constitution offers Social economic and political Justice. Justice is the quality of being just; fairness. It is the principle of moral rightness; equity. It is the Conformity to moral rightness in action or attitude; righteousness.

The *Directive Principles of State Policy* are guidelines to the central and state governments of India, to be kept in mind while framing laws and policies. These provisions, contained in Part IV of the Constitution of India, are not enforceable by any court, but the principles laid down therein are considered fundamental in the governance of the country, making it the duty of the State to apply these principles in making laws to establish a just society in the country. The principles have been inspired by the Directive Principles given in the Constitution of Ireland and also by the principles of Gandhism; and relate to social justice, economic welfare, foreign policy, and legal and administrative matters. Directive Principles are classified under the following categories: Gandhian, economic and socialistic, political and administrative, justice and legal, environmental, protection of monuments and peace and security.

Justice is a concept of moral rightness based on ethics, rationality, law, natural law, religion, equity or fairness, as well as the administration of the law, taking into account the inalienable and inborn rights of all human beings and citizens, the right of all people and individuals to equal protection before the law of their civil rights, without discrimination on the basis of race, gender, sexual orientation, gender identity, national origin, colour, ethnicity, religion, disability, age, or other characteristics, and is further regarded as being inclusive of social justice.

According to most contemporary theories of justice, justice is overwhelmingly important: John Rawls claims that "Justice is the first virtue of social institutions, as truth is of systems of thought". Justice can be thought of as distinct from and more fundamental than benevolence, charity, mercy, generosity, or compassion. Justice has traditionally been associated with concepts of fate, reincarnation or Divine Providence, *i.e.*, with a life in accordance with the cosmic plan. The association of justice with fairness has thus been historically and culturally rare and is perhaps chiefly a modern innovation [in western societies].

Liberty

Indian constitution offers Liberty of thought, expression, belief, faith and worship. Liberty is the value of individuals to have agency (control over their own actions). Different conceptions of liberty articulate the relationship of individuals to society in different ways – including some that relate to life under a social contract or to existence in a state of nature, and some that see the active exercise of freedom and rights as essential to liberty. Understanding liberty involves how we imagine the individual's roles and responsibilities in society in relation to concepts of free will and determinism, which involves the larger domain of metaphysics.

Individualist and classical liberal conceptions of liberty typically consist of the freedom of individuals from outside compulsion or coercion, also known as negative liberty. This conception of liberty, which coincides with the libertarian point-of-view, suggests that people should, must, and ought to behave according to their own free will, and take responsibility for their actions, while in contrast, Social liberal conceptions of (positive liberty) liberty place an emphasis upon social structure and agency and is therefore directed toward ensuring egalitarianism. In feudal societies, a 'liberty' was an area of allodial land where the rights of the ruler or monarch were waived.

Equality

Indian constitution guarantees Equality of status and of opportunity, and promote among all the citizens of India. The six fundamental rights recognised by the constitution are:

1. Right to equality, including equality before law, prohibition of discrimination on grounds of religion, race, caste, sex or place of birth, and equality of opportunity in matters of employment, abolition of un-touchability and abolition of titles.
2. Right to freedom which includes speech and expression, assembly, association or union or co-operatives, movement, residence, and right to practice any profession or occupation (some of these rights are subject to security of the State, friendly relations with foreign countries, public order, decency or morality), right to life and liberty, right to education, protection in respect to conviction in offences and protection against arrest and detention in certain cases.

3. Right against exploitation, prohibiting all forms of forced labour, child labour and traffic in human beings.
4. Right to freedom of religion, including freedom of conscience and free profession, practice, and propagation of religion, freedom to manage religious affairs, freedom from certain taxes and freedom from religious instructions in certain educational institutes.
5. Cultural and Educational rights preserving Right of any section of citizens to conserve their culture, language or script, and right of minorities to establish and administer educational institutions of their choice.
6. Right to constitutional remedies for enforcement of Fundamental Rights. Fundamental rights for Indians have also been aimed at overturning the inequalities of pre-independence social practices. Specifically, they have also been used to abolish untouchability and hence prohibit discrimination on the grounds of religion, race, caste, sex, or place of birth. They also forbid trafficking of human beings and forced labour. They also protect cultural and educational rights of ethnic and religious minorities by allowing them to preserve their languages and also establish and administer their own education institutions. Right to property was originally a fundamental right, but is now a legal right.

Fraternity

Indian constitution guarantees Fraternity, assuring the dignity of the individual and the unity and integrity of the nation. A sense of fraternity is assured the dignity of the individual and the unity of the nation. The basic principles of democracy are, justice, liberty, equality and fraternity.

A fraternity (Latin*frater*: 'brother') is a brotherhood, although the term sometimes connotes a distinct or formal organization and sometimes a secret society. A fraternity (or fraternal organization) is an organized society of men associated together in an environment of companionship and brotherhood; dedicated to the intellectual, physical, and social development of its members.

REFERENCE

1. Ismail Thamarasseri (2007), *Education in the Emerging Indian Society*. New Delhi: Kanishka Publishers.
2. Ismail Thamarasseri (2013), *Philosophical Foundations of Education*. Agra: Sri Vinod Pustak Mandir.
3. http://en.wikipedia.org/wiki/Sovereignty

9 Educational Exclusion and Inclusive Development in India

Educational achievements in India remain wanting in the current century, after sixty odd years of independence. While the Indian constitution has deemed education to be a fundamental right the reality on the ground is that only 81.1 per cent of youth and 62.8 per cent of adults are deemed to be literate (UNESCO 2008).

The lackluster educational profile of India provided by national statistics is further emphasised when placed in relation to the global goals endorsed at the end of the twentieth century. The commitment to Education for All (EFA), first enunciated at the Jomtien Declaration 1990, and the achievement of Universal Primary Education (UPE) set out as a Millennium Development Goal to be achieved by 2015 appear to be unattainable within the context of the educational policies adopted by the Indian state (GOI 2005).

Achieving education policy can be analysed in terms of both the consistency of the stated objectives as well as in relation to the financial outlays and adminstrative resources allocated to ensure the successful implementation of educational policy. In this regard, the educational policies of the government of the United Progress Alliance (UPA), comprising the Congress party and its alliance with the Left parties, the Samajvadi Party, and the Bahujan Samaj Party, after the general elections of 2004 had set out its objectives in the Common Minimum Programme adopted on the 29th of May, 2004.

The main plank of the CMP was a political promise to reverse the communalisation of the Indian education system that had been brought in by the previous government, the National Democratic Alliance, led by BJP. This objective was to be met by ensuring that all institutions of higher learning were able to 'retain their autonomy' as this was seen to be under threat during the previous regime. The reversal was also to be brought about through the appointment of a review committee of experts to ensure a removal of communalised aspects of the school syllabus that had been brought in by the NDA government. In relation to the school system the CMP identified the mid-day meal (MDM) scheme as the major programme to be introduced into primary and secondary school as a way to improve the performance of the educational sector. It additionally announced that it would work to universalise education in the primary sector and ensure full coverage of education for early years under the ICDS scheme. On the financial side, the CMP underlined that it would spend at least the recommended 6 per cent of public spending on education and that at the very minimum half of this expenditure would be on the primary and secondary sectors. Additionally, The consistency of policy objectives has been an established criteria for assessment has been in place since the celebrated work of Jan Tinbergen in the 1960s.

These key components of the UPA's commitment need to be analysed in relation to both the relative success in implementing educational policy in furthering the agenda of Education for All as well as with regard to the ability of such an educational policy to ensure a socially transformative development process.

Financing Education

There has been a long-standing demand for the provision of six per cent of the national budget for education going back to the recommendations of the Kothari Commission Report of 1964. The percentage of India's GNP allocated to education in 2005-06 was 3.7 per cent. This increase is marginally an improvement on the amount allocated to elementary education in 2003-04 of 1.8 per cent (Tilak 2009). The latest statistics indicate that 10.7 per cent of government spending went to education in 2007 and of this 36 per cent went to the primary sector. It is clear that government expenditure is a far smaller amount than the Gross National Product and while the former figure shows that the share of spending is moving closer to 5 per cent the latter figure remains close to 2 per cent. The share of public expenditure going to education was 10.7 per cent and not significantly different from the percentages spent under the NDA (Fennell 2006).

Stewart (2009) points out that a state unable to ensure service delivery should be deemed to have failed. In this sense, the Indian state and consistently being unable to ensure educational outlays of the order of 6 per cent of the GDP, and should be regarded as failing in some sense.

On the other hand, while there has been a manifest inability to meet the expenditure levels recommended by previous commissions set up by the Indian government there has been an increase in the expenditure allocations for elementary education in recent plans: the 8th plan (1992-97) allocated 406,00 (Rs. Million), there was 147,500 (Rs. Million) in the 9th Plan (1997-2002) and an allocation of 287,500 (Rs. Million) for the 10th Plan (2002-07) and 275,000 (Rs. Million) in the 11th Plan (2007-13). The expenditure on education by both central and state education departments was 2.81 per cent of GDP in 2005-06, with half the amount going in elementary education (Tilak 2009). Additionally, while the revenue collected by the levy of the 2 per cent cess was Rs. 7,036 crores the budget outlay for elementary education was only over half that amount.

The outright failure of the UPA government to ensure that its own stated objective of 'at least six per cent of its GNP' being allocated to education indicates its inability to make good its political promises. The contrast between the high political priority accorded to education in the CMP and the low level of additional finances made available for educational policies does beg the question of whether the UPA had given serious thought to devising a educational policy that be able to ensure universal elementary education (UEE).

To explore whether the financial shortfall was a consequence of merely inadequate resource mobilisation or more serious shortcomings in policy-making we turn to an evaluation of educational policy during the UPA's term in office.

Situating the Education Policy of the UPA

The educational objectives set out in the CMP fall far short of a new framework for achieving national or international goals. The major objective of the CMP of removing the communal aspects of educational policy while an important political platform for the UPA does not set out any new policies, limiting itself to the establishment of a review panel of experts to rectify the communalisation of the school syllabus. The only clear objective outlined in the CMP, with regard to the educational sector, was achieving the objective of universal basic education, largely through the greater coverage of the midday meal scheme in schools. The greater emphasis on a political agenda rather than the setting out of a clear cut educational policy in the CMP appears to corroborate the view that Indian policy-making is increasingly becoming more about gaining political legitimacy rather than ensuring financial resources (Mooij 2007).

The objective of achieving universal primary education set out in the CMP was not a definitive policy agenda in itself but rather a furthering of existing educational policies of previous governments to extend educational coverage, such as the District Primary Education Programme (DPEP) that was introduced in 1994 with the objectives of providing universal access to school. This programme was incorporated into a larger national level educational policy in 2000-01, covering all India's districts, under the aegis of the Sarva Shiksha Abhiyan (SSA). The SSA had the ambitious objective of ensuring universal primary education by 2007 and was initially based on an 85:15 financial outlay by central and state government during the period of the 10th plan.

The mid-term review of the MDGs indicate that India was moving towards UPE with 95 per cent children enrolled in primary school but the retention levels till grade five are just 79 per cent in 2005 (UNESCO 2008). While the overall objective of UPE might appear to be in sight there were concerns expressed regarding the meeting of associated Millennium goals of gender parity, as the Gender Parity Index (GPI) has not been attained, and the figure was 0.94 in 2005. The data does cast some doubt on the ability of the SSA to deliver educational policy at the local level, through the district and muncipal authorities respectively, in rural and urban India. The tools of the SSA for ensuring complete enrolment and retention, as well as the target of gender parity, through specific programme interventions to target groups, as the poor households and the education of girls do not appear to have delivered adequately.

Furthermore, there was little attempt during the UPA term in office to devise a detailed financial plan for ensuring educational delivery. In particular, the additional financial outlays at state and local level to deliver these programmes were set out within the guidelines of the existing 10th plan, where educational provision was to be based on a financial sharing on a 50:50 basis between the centre and the states. This arrangement was based on a strict financial proviso, whereby the state governments could be denied annual plan funds if they failed to transfer their contributions to the State Implementation Committee for the previous year. There was no indication in the CMP of 2004 that there would be any change in these financial arrangements to ensure that target of UPE, that was not achieved as originally envisaged by 2007, would now be achieved during its term of office. The only additional funds to be obtained was through the imposition of an educational cess of 2 per cent on all central taxes to provide funds to help achieve the objective of universal primary education and this was to be put towards funding the MDM scheme in schools.

Mid-Day Meal Scheme as an Educational Programme

The MDM scheme announced by the UPA government in 2004 as its main initiative to attain universal primary education was not in itself a new policy. In fact, the scheme was the consequence of a court directive in response to a writ petition filed in the Supreme Court of India in 2001 to demand India's food stocks be used to prevent hunger. It was the interim order of the Court, on 28th November 2001, that directed all state governments to provide children in government and government assisted schools a prepared mid-day meal as a measure to relieve 'classroom hunger' (Dreze and Goyal 2003). Throughout the following year, there were concerted attempts by NGOs to monitor the implementation of the MDM scheme which revealed that the initial financial outlay fell far short of the requirement to provide meals of an adequate quality. So rather than being a new focus, the MDM emerges from a set of legal and lobbying battles to ensure the 'right to food', and thereby to guarantee that Article 21 of the Indian Constitution on the 'right to life', as the driver for the MDM scheme (Khera 2005). There is little indication in the CMP that the MDM was to play a part in a larger educational policy framework to achieve national and international educational objectives.

The *Report to the People* released on the third anniversary of the UPA also emphasises the importance of targetted funds for improving the educational attainments of minority and deprived groups.

The recent PROBE study conducted in 2006 does show that midday meals were an important feature in increasing access and attendance (Samson 2008?). This finding is contradictory to the international financial institutions (IFI) view that targeted programmes are more effective as they focus on the most disadvantaged rather than providing a generalised subsidy (King *et al.*, 1997).

The incentives are effective when they work through with by poor and marginalised groups to overcome obstacles to accessing education.

Schemes such as the MDM act by providing incentives for parents to send their children to school (Jayaram 2008). The increased attraction of schools due to the provision of a hot cooked meal is particularly relevant for the most economically disadvantaged sectors, where malnourishment of children is an endemic condition. Consequently, a MDM scheme could ensure both increased enrolment in schools as well as improved attention of children from the most deprived sections of society. Improvement in both attendance and the increased socialisation at school are also achieved by incentive schemes such as the provision of free textbooks and the awarding of scholarships for girls.

The evidence regarding the effectiveness of these schemes is mixed, with some studies pointing out that the universal schemes (*e.g.*, mid-day meals and textbooks) perform better than targeted schemes (*e.g.*, scholarships for girls). While the studies recognise that leakages do persist, they find evidence that these are considerably reduced through improved monitoring of the programme to ensure that the food does arrive at the school and is of an adequate quality (Samson, Noronha and De 2008). The research indicates that with increased transparency and awareness-raising measures put in place there could also be an improved attendance level in response to other school incentives such as uniforms and free text-books (Khera, Samson and De 2009).

The introduction of specific programmes that target the socially under privileged and discriminated categories, such as gender, minority status, and disability have been applauded by international bodies (EFA GMR 2008). It is noteworthy, that in the case of India, universal programmes that cover all government and government aided schools, such as MDM, have also been effective when administered effectively by the school authorities though this might not reduce the gender gap, as both girls and boys appear to benefit equally for the programme (Jayaram 2008). The key seems to lie in the ability to make the explicit link between educational inputs, the process of educational service delivery and the type of educational outcome that results from such a programme (Pritchett and Pande 2006).

The flipside of this finding is that it cannot be presumed that funding of an educational programme within the ongoing framework of the SSA, is an automatic guarantee for ensuring UPE. Achieving UPE requires an understanding of the process of educational delivery and its implication for the nature and extent of successful educational outcomes. Programmes to improve educational outcomes must consequently operate within a social context that favours children from more disadvantaged and discriminated groups attending and completing school. The provision for MDM and other school based incentives are therefore most effective where there is widespread community level support for all children being at school, *i.e.*, full support for the principle of the 'right to education' (Khera, Samson and De 2009). If school programmes are undertaken in an environment where social stratification, particularly caste distinctions, then they are unlikely to be able to ensure equal treatment of all school children and their 'right to education'.

Despite contemporary evidence that institutional mechanisms should be based on every child's right to education the CMP does not indicate that the programmatic aspects, such as MDM and ICDS, are working within such constitutional requirements for the provision of education. The absence of any explicit indication of how the legislative framework would be linked to the revised educational policy indicate that interrelations between institutional reform and programme implementation were not considered at the outset of UPA's term in office.

This appears strange given the discernable shifts in public opinion on the 'right to education'. following the awarding of landmark legal judgements in the 1990s (the most significant being *Unnikrishan, J.P., vs. The State of Andhra Pradesh*) with regard to the interpretation of the right to education as a constitutional right. The legal judgement and the public interest that resulted led to the formation of a national coalition, National Association for the Fundamental Right to Education (NAFRE), and a campaign for the recognition of education as a fundamental right. The demands made by civil society organizations pushing for a bill in the Lok Sabha resulted in the passing of the 86th Constitutional Ammendment (Article 21A) in 2002 that required the state to provide free and compulsory education till the age of fourteen. Despite these major legal achievements in the preceeding years the CMP did not directly mention how it would meet the additional costs of financing of ensuring such a legal obligation nor does it refer to the 'right to education' directly.

There was also no reference, in the CMP, to the particular design of an educational programme that would directly remedy the fallings of the SSA in achieving UPE. This further suggests that the UPA had not thought deep and hard about the specific educational outcomes that it wished to realise when it came to power in 2004. The UPA's willingness to focus solely on programmes, largely on the MDM, as a tool to accelerate universal primary education points to a lack of any premediated thinking on financial and administrative requirements to ensure improved educational outcomes.

The consequences of the limited remit of the UPA is also evident in its own *Report to the People* released at the third anniversary of the alliance's victory in the national polls which identifies its major objectives and achievements in the field of education. The report profiled the increase in the expenditure outlays as the pathway to success in moving towards education for all, particularly the achievement of 96 per cent of habitations having access to a primary school and that the MDM was the biggest feeding programme in the world and covered 115 million children in primary and primary aided schools (GOI 2008). It did not make any reference to the method of financial provisioning for the final mile towards UPE. While the increased demographic coverage by educational programmes is a positive feature, this is in a context where India still accounted for 21 million of the 72 million out of school children in the world in 2008 (UNESCO

GMR 2008) and yet there was no underlining of the need to place the legal responsibility of the state at the centre of educational provision despite the voluble discussion in the public sphere regarding the legal obligation to uphold the constitutional right to education.

The Institutional and Legal Processes in Education

The central message emerging from the CMF was the need to remedy the saffronisation of education that took place under the NDA government. It was in pursuance of this obective that the UPA government reconstituted the Central Advisory Board for Education (CABE) on the 6th of July 2004. Authorising the CABE to review and make recommendations thorough key committees put into motion a number of processes by which the legal, institutional and curricular aspects of educational policy would come into play.

The first meeting of the reconstituted CABE was held in August 2004 and its members, drawn from both houses of parliament as well as experts for the worlds of academia and public life, identified key areas that needed 'detailed deliberations' and the setting up of the specific committees to deal with these areas. The MHRD provided a detailed term of reference for each committee, and reports were submitted by each committee with the key policy recommendations that were required to ensure the achievement of each objective (MHRD 2004, 200.

The committee reports examine the relationship of education policy with development, both in relation to economic success as well as social justice. The recommendations of the committees indicate that very careful consideration was given to both academic arguments as well as legal judgements regarding the position of education in India's development. Nor were the individual committees averse to expanding their individual remit, and the Committee for girls's education recommended that 'alongside the 86th Amendment the Government of India bring in another Act to protect the fundamental right to life of the child in the form of the right to live in a civil society with full provision by the state of both primary health needs and early educational care for children up to 6 years.' (GOI 2005b: 9).

The principle that the provision of education should be based on the principle of social justice and ensure equality for all children was evident in the recommendations of the committee on girls' education and inclusion. The report repeatedly underlined the necessity for a common school system that was both state-funded and state-led if the education system was to ensure the inclusion of all children.

Achieving UEE and the Agenda of Inclusive Development

The limitations of policy and finance that have figured prominently as reasons for the lack of a fully-fledged educational policy do not only mar the educational objectives of the UPA government but also cast doubts on the ability of the government to pursue a distinctive pattern of development. This is particularly the case as the UPA has made a series of public statements regarding its intention to set out a new and more socially transformative path to development, than that followed by previous governments.

The Prime Ministers' Independence Day speech in 2006 emphasised the need to send all children to school and reiterated that the SSA and the MDM would be the government's initiatives to achieve this objective.

'The expanded Sarva Shiksha Abhiyan will ensure that all our children go to school. Under the universal Mid-day Meal Programme, almost 12 crore children are getting a nutritious meal at school. Through these two programmes, we will ensure that all our children complete basic schooling'.

The almost identical language in the CMP of 2004 and the speech of 2006, without any mention of a new directive, and no allusion to changes in educational policy beg the question of why there was no evidence of responses to the vociferous public debates in the preceding years. The absence is also surprising given the importance accorded to the empowering aspect of education in the UPA agenda.

On the third anniversary of the UPA government, May 22nd 2007, the Prime Minister stated that a strategy of development that was based on 'inclusive growth', was superior to following a purely growth oriented strategy as it combined empowerment, with entitlement and investment. The major contribution to be made by the provision of public goods through public investment was spelt out of very clearly in this statement.

'Education empowers, improved health care empowers, employment guarantee entitles, fulfilling quota obligations entitles. Through a combination of offering entitlement, ensuring empowerment and stepping up public investment, our Government has sought to make the growth process more inclusive.'

There is a stark contrast between the vision conjoured up by these words of an education policy that would ensure that all children are getting a quality education and inability to realise the objective of Universal Elementary Education as the financing of education continues to fall short of the required level of six per cent of GDP. Furthermore, an adequate financial outlay might not be a sufficient condition for ensuring universal primary education, even though it is a necessary condition (Alston and Bhuna 2005). *Thirdly*, the programmes that have been successful in increasing enrolment and retention, such as MDM, do not by themselves ensure the delivery of a quality education and are successful only in environments where institutional mechanisms are based on tenets of equality and social justice. These shortcomings in meeting the UPA's own objective of UPE are not explicitly recognised in the 11th plan.

The 11th plan documents do trace a linkage between the UPA's development strategy of 'inclusive growth', the major plank for government planning between 2007-12, and the objectives of the CMP announced by the UPA during the course of the 10th plan. However, there does not appear to be any new and distinctive educational policy emerging from the objectives of the CMP. If education is to have a central role in relation to achieving 'inclusive growth' there needs to be a fundamental rethinking on the provisioning of education. In particular, there must be a commitment that the legal responsibility of the state is to be met with adequate financial resources to ensure *(a)* that right to education is made available to all children as demanded by the courts and *(b)* the greater consideration to taken of importance of both content of education and context within which education is provided as recommended by expert committees of the CABE.

The new development paradigm of inclusive growth cannot be met by incremental increases in individual programmes alone. If empowerment through education is to be the way forward then considerable financial resources need to be expended on the educational sector (at the very least the six per cent that has been a long-standing recommendation). These resources must also firmly linked to an educational policy that has an established set of procedures for public consultation which will result in negotiation and consensus of the principles and processes to ensure UEE and other national educational goals.

The power of education cannot be unleased if there is dissipation of human energies, those of expert bodies, public figures, professionals and civil society organizations, on account of a lack of institutional processes to harness the best of civil society initiatives and government legislation. Educational exclusion will continue as a social mechanisms unless there is the embedding of a set of institutional practices that work with social norms and community practices (Fennell 2010) to ensure that children complete education in inclusive school environments.

REFERENCE

1. Shailaja Fennell (October 2010), Educational *Exclusion and Inclusive Development in India.* Department of International Development. Research Consortium on Educational Outcomes and Poverty.

Gender Differences in Education

Children's School Attendance – at a Glance

- Only two-thirds of girls and three-fourths of boys' age 6-17 years are attending school. The sex ratio of children attending school is 889 girls per 1,000 boys.
- There is gender equality in school attendance in urban areas; but, in rural areas, the female disadvantage in education is marked and increases with age.
- Age-appropriate school attendance is lower than any school attendance for both boys and girls. However, boys and girls who are in school are about equally likely to be in an age-inappropriate class.
- School dropout beyond primary school is a major problem for both girls and boys.

Literacy and Educational Attainment among Adults

- The percentage of adults who are literate is much lower in rural than in urban areas; none the less, even in urban areas one-fourth of women and more than one tenth of men are not literate. Gender disparity in literacy is much greater in rural than in urban areas and declines sharply with household wealth.

- Forty-one per cent of women and 18 per cent of men age 15-49 have never been to school.
- Educational attainment remains very low: even among the 20-29 age group, only 27 per cent of women and 39 per cent of men have 10 or more years of education.
- The percentage of ever-married women with 10 or more years of education has risen very slowly from 11 per cent in NFHS-1 to 17 per cent in NFHS-3.

Eliminating gender differences in access to education and educational attainment are key elements on the path to attaining gender equality and reducing the disempowerment of women. In recognition of the pivotal role of education in development and of persistent gender inequalities in access to education, the elimination of gender disparity in primary education is one of the Millennium Development Goals. The achievement of universal primary education has been a key goal of Indian planning since Independence. However, increasing access to primary schooling still leaves the twin questions of educational quality and school retention unanswered. Continued economic development cannot be sustained with a population that has merely completed primary school; it needs adepend able supply of highly educated and skilled human capital for which a high level of educational attainment of both women and men is necessary. However, ensuring a continued supply of skilled human capital to sustain economic growth is only one objective of reducing gender inequalities in educational attainment: the other is that education, particularly higher education of women, is a key enabler of demographic change, family welfare, and better health and nutrition of women and their families. Higher education has the potential to empower women with knowledge and ways of understanding and manipulating the world around them. Education of women has been shown to be associated with lower fertility, infant mortality, and better child health and nutrition. The analysis of children's school attendance is based on their attendance at any time during the 2005-06 school years. To increase accuracy and comparability, children's ages are adjusted to the start of the 2005-06 school year assumed hereto be April 2005.

School Attendance of Children Age 6-17 Years: Levels and Differentials

An examination of the data on school attendance by age, however, reveals that gender disparity in school attendance is largely a rural phenomenon. In urban areas, about equal proportions of boys and girls attend school at each age; however, in rural areas, gender inequality in attendance is evident in every age group and increases with age. Notably, even in urban areas, only about half the children age 15-17 attend school. Both supply and demand-side factors play a role in whether children attend school or not. Key supply-side factors include the availability, accessibility, and quality of schools – factors for which no information is available in NFHS-3. The demand-side factors include the level of education of household members and household wealth – factors whose influence can be examined using NFHS-3 data. Adults who are educated are more likely to ensure that their children are educated. Wealth enables access to education by providing the resources needed to buy quality education and by reducing the opportunity cost of children's time. For poorer households, children's time spent in school is time not spent in contributing to the economic sustainability of the household.

School Attendance by Education of Household Head

School attendance at all ages and for both boys and girls increases with the education level of the household head. Among all children age 6-17, only 53 per cent of girls and 65 per cent of boys attended school in 2005-06 if they belonged to a household with an uneducated head of household. By contrast, 9 out of 10 boys and girls attended school if they belonged to a household where the head had 12 or more years of education. It is also notable that belonging to a household in which the household head has a high level of education is associated with higher educational attainment for the next generation: almost three out of four children age

15-17 in households where the household head has 12 or more years of education were attending school, compared with the national average of 35 per cent for girls and 48 per cent for boys age 15-17. Gender differentials in school attendance decline sharply as the educational level of the household head increases. The differentials are particularly notable for the age-group 15-17: in this age group, the sex ratio of children (females per 1,000 males) attending school increases from a low of 546 in households with an uneducated household head to 900 in households with a household head who has at least 12 years of education.

School Attendance by Household Wealth

School attendance also increases sharply by the wealth status of households. The data suggest that belonging to a household in the lowest wealth quintile is associated with even lower rates of school attendance at every age than belonging to a household where the household head is uneducated. In addition, gender inequality in school attendance also varies more sharply by wealth in every age group than it does by education of the household head. The greatest variation in the sex ratio (females per 1,000 males) of children attending school by wealth is for the age-group 15-17: in this age group, the sex ratio of those attending school increases from a low of 426 inhouseholds belonging to the lowest wealth quintile to 936 in households belonging to the highest wealth quintile.

School Attendance by State

The sex ratio (girls per 1,000 boys) of children age 6-17 who attended school in the 2005-06 school year ranges from 745 in Rajasthan and Bihar to 1,081 in Meghalaya. There are nine states where the sex ratio of children attending school is less than 900, 16 states where the ratio is 900-999 and four states where the proportion of girls attending school is more than the proportion of boys attending school. These results suggest that, despite the variation across states in the proportion of children attending school, gender equality in school attendance has been attained in some states and is close to being attained in several other states. States where gender equality in school attendance is close to being attained stretch from the south and west of India, through the centre into the north, with several states in the northeast also falling in this group.

Age Appropriate School Attendance

Examining school attendance of children by age does not tell us whether children are beginning school at the right age (considered to be age 6 years in India) and are progressing from class to class in an age-appropriate manner. The net attendance rate (NAR) and the gross attendance rate (GAR) are measures of age-appropriate school attendance. These rates are defined separately for the primary and secondary levels of education as follows:

- *For Primary School:* NAR: Children age 6-10 years in classes 1-5 as a proportion of all children age 6-10 years GAR: All children in classes 1-5 as a proportion of all children age 6-10 years.
- *For Secondary School:* NAR: Children age 11-17 years in classes 6-12 as a proportion of children age 11-17 years GAR: All children in classes 6-12 as a proportion of all children age 11-17 years.

Gender Differentials in Adult Literacy

Literacy, *i.e.*, the ability to read and write, is the foundation of education. NFHS-3 shows that only 55 per cent of women and 78 per cent of men are literate in India. Literacy has, however, been increasing over time for both women and men as measured by changes across age groups. In fact, literacy among women is almost twice as high in the 15-19 age group than in the age-group 45-49 that is 30 year solder. None the less, even in the youngest age group, one in four women and one in ten men are not literate. Although the gender differential in literacy has declined over time, the differential remains high even in the youngest age group: among those 15-19 years of age, the percentage off males who are literate (74%) is 15 percentage points less than the percentage of males who are literate (89%). Notably, the differential by residence for women is much greater than for men (29 percentage points for women *vs.* 16 for men) and the gender disparity in literacy is also much greater in rural than in urban areas. None the less, even in urban areas, one-fourth of women are not literate. In the lowest wealth quintile, only 19 per cent of women are literate, compared with 47 per cent of men. However, literacy increases sharply with wealth and the increase for women is greater than for men. Consequently, the gender differential in literacy narrows rapidly with wealth, so that in the highest wealth quintile, 90 per cent of women are literate, compared with 97 per cent of men.

Trends in Educational Attainment

Trends in educational attainment can be examined by looking at changes across age cohorts or at data from multiple time points collected using the same questions. The proportion of ever-married women age 15-49 that have 10 or more years of education in each of the three NFHS surveys. This comparison of educational attainment is restricted to ever married women since never married women were not interviewed in NFHS-1and NFHS-.

The educational attainment of a sample of ever-married women is not representative of all women since the more educated women in the younger age cohorts, particularly the 15-19 and 20-24 cohorts, are less likely to be married and, hence, will be under-represented in this sample. None the less, a sample of ever-married women serves well in representing the women currently bearing and rearing children and making reproductive health and nutritional decisions.

REFERENCE

1. Sunita Kishor and Kamla Gupta (August 2009), Gender Equality and Women's Empowerment in India. *Ministry of Health and Family Welfare*, Government of India.
2. National Family Health Survey (NFHS-3), India, 2005-06.

Socialism and its Educational Implications

Socialism

Is an economic system characterised by social ownership of the means of production and co-operative management of the economy. 'Social ownership' may refer to co-operative enterprises, common ownership, state ownership, citizen ownership of equity, or any combination of these. There are many varieties of socialism and there is no single definition encapsulating all of them. They differ in the type of social ownership they advocate, the degree to which they rely on markets or planning, how management is to be organized within productive institutions, and the role of the state in constructing socialism.

A socialist economic system consists of a system of production and distribution organized to directly satisfy economic demands and human needs, so that goods and services are produced directly for use instead of for private profit driven by the accumulation of capital. Accounting is based on physical quantities, a common physical magnitude, or a direct measure of labour-time in place of financial calculation. Distribution is based on the principle to each according to his contribution. Marxist theory holds that the development of the socialist mode of production will give rise to a communist society, in which classes and the state are no longer present, there is access abundance to final goods, and thus distribution is based on to each according to his need.

As a political movement, socialism includes a diverse array of political philosophies, ranging from reformism to revolutionary socialism. Proponents of state socialism advocate the nationalisation of the means of production, distribution and exchange as a strategy for implementing socialism. In contrast, libertarian socialism opposes the use of state power to achieve such an arrangement, opposing both parliamentary politics and state ownership. Democratic socialism seeks to establish socialism through democratic processes and propagate its ideals within the context of a democratic political system.

Modern socialism originated from an 18th-century intellectual and working class political movement that criticised the effects of industrialisation and private property on society. In the early 19th-century, 'socialism' referred to any concern for the social problems of capitalism irrespective of the solutions to those problems. However, by the late 19th-century, 'socialism' had come to signify opposition to capitalism and advocacy for an alternative system based on some form of social ownership. Marxists expanded further on this, attributing scientific assessment and democratic planning as critical elements of socialism.

As an economic and political philosophy, socialism began as an attack on the concepts of private property and personal profit. These aspects of capitalism, socialists believed, should be replaced by public ownership of property and sharing profits. Robert Owen in England, Henri de Saint Simon (France) and in 19th century Karl Marx (USSR) is the proponents of socialism. Karl Marx observed, socialist state must be controlled by working class.

Definition

"An economic philosophy based on the concept of public ownership of property and sharing of profits, together with the belief that economic decision should be controlled by the workers". – William Kornblum, 1998.

Meaning

Socialism has its origin in Europe as a revolt against capitalism in the 19th century. Its salient ideas spread all over the world. These are different brands/forms or socialism especially those shared by Karl Marx Lenin in Russia, Mao in China and Gandhi in India.

In 1947 in an editorial under the caption 'who is a socialist' Gandhi wrote, "under socialism all the members of the society are equal-none low, none high .....Even as members or the individual body are equal, so are the members of the society. This is socialism, under it, the prince and the peasant, the wealthy and the poor, the employer and the employee are all on the same level".

Socialism is a scheme of social organization, which places the means of production and distribution in the hands of the community. Socialism is part and parcel of the concept of the welfare state. By planning and fully utilising all the resources available in the country, it seeks to provide maximum benefit to all the people".

Characteristics/Features

- Socialism aims at social justice.
- It aims at equality.
- It aims a class less society, free from exploitation, oppression and disparity.
- It pre-supposes public ownership of the means of production.
- It aims at active participation of the individual in the productive process of society.
- It aims at establishing a society based on mental co-operation and fellow feeling.

- It aims at abolishing the capitalist system.
- It aims at developing necessary skills and favourable attitudes towards work.

Indian Constitution and Socialism

The 42nd constitutional amendment on 1976 the term socialism included in our constitution; unto that it implicit in 4th chapter, directive principles of state policy. Based on the implicit/hidden one our parliament accepts the idea of 'socialistic pattern of society' in 1954. In economy we stand between capitalism and socialism *i.e.*, mixed economy. We aim a democratic socialist nation. We keep both socialist ideals and basic human rights.

Friends, but what's the present condition? Our great aim, classes less society still a myth even after 60 years of independence. Equality between man and man is a far reaching objective. In democracy, we are trying to uphold uniqueness. But it doesn't go parallel with universality/ socialism. This conflict leads liberal democracy and extending freedom. 80 per cent wealth accumulated on 20 per cent of population. It's not only the issue of India but also all over the world. In our democracy, welfare of the majority is the welfare of the all, *i.e.*, if 51 per cent of people have food, that equal to nation have food.

Educational Implications of Socialism

Aims of Education and Socialism, Emphasis on

- Social development of an individual.
- Education for citizenship.
- Socialisation of the individual.

Contents/Curriculum

- More emphasis on core curriculum.
- Subject matter stressing equality.
- Study of socialistic movements.
- Socially useful productive work and work experience.

Methods of Teaching

- Socialized recitation techniques.
- Project method.

- Problem method.
- Team teaching.

Educational Measures for Promoting a Socialist Society

Kothari commission observed, "one of the important social objectives of education is to equalise opportunity, enabling the backward or under privilaged classes and individuals to use education as a lever for the improvement of their condition. Every society that values social justice and is anxious to improve the lot of the common man and cultivate all available talent, must ensure progressive equality of opportunity to all section of population. This is the only guarantee for the building up of an egalitarian and human society in which the exploitation of the weak will be minimized".

Teaching of Socialism

It is the responsibility of the educational institutions to bring about adequate awareness regarding socialism among the teachers and students so that the young people are armed with knowledge which will enable them to chart the course of the nation towards the goal of socialism. The following are three main ways in which a school can convey positive attitudes and values regarding socialism to students:

1. Direct teaching of socialism.
2. Living the values and attitudes to be learned through the organization of various activities.
3. Teachers becoming models embodying the desired values and attitudes.

Text Books and Socialism

As an impact of socialism, text-books at the school stage, by and large, have been nationalised. The contents of text-books are oriented and regulated according to the national policy and ethos. Efforts are being made to keep the price range of text books within the easy reach of the parents.

Equality of Opportunity in Education

The Kothari Commission observed, "On grounds of social justice as well as for the furtherance of democracy it is essential to make special efforts to equalise educational opportunities between these groups".

Ways and Means of Providing Equality of Opportunity in Education

- Tuition fee education to economically weaker sections of students.
- Free textbooks and informs to the weaker sections.
- Establishment of book banks.
- Award of scholarship.
- Granting of loans.
- Day-study centres and lodging houses.
- Earn and learn facilities.
- Special facilities for girls.
- Special stress on the education of the backward sections of societies-tribals, slum areas, hilly areas etc.
- Meeting the needs of slow learners and the handicapped.
- Running and maintenance and state/government schools.
- Equality of opportunity in admission.
- Common school system.

REFERENCES

1. Ismail Thamarasseri (2007), *Education in the Emerging Indian Society*, New Delhi: Kanishka Publishers.
2. Http://en.wikipedia.org/wiki/Socialism

Education of the Differently Abled

Inclusive Education

Historically, attempts towards development and ensuring equality and justice for all have commonly been found to conform to the norms and systems of the majority. Most of these attempts have articulated the need for inclusion of all segments of the society – however, in most cases this articulation took the form of 'special care systems' that ultimately led to further exclusion of these communities – physically, mentally and psychologically. For a variegated and multi-segment society like India it is even more common. Common School System (CSS) that has as its bedrock the principles of equality, justice and inclusion.

Common School System (CSS) has been defined from varied perspectives reflecting on the diverse backgrounds, knowledge base, skills, concepts, ideologies and experiences of people and institutions involved. An attempt to provide a comprehensive definition of CSS was made while proposing to the CABE Committee on 'Free and Compulsory Education' as follows – 'Common School System means the National System of Education that is founded on the principles of equality and social justice as enshrined in the Constitution and provides education of a comparable quality to all children in an equitable manner irrespective of their caste, creed, language, gender, economic or ethnic background, location or disability (physical or mental), and wherein all categories of schools – *i.e.*, government, local body or private, both aided and unaided, or otherwise – will be obliged to:

(a) Fulfill certain minimum infrastructural (including those relating to teachers and other staff), financial, curricular, pedagogic, linguistic and socio-cultural norms.

(b) Ensure free education to the children in a specified neighbourhood from an age group and/or up to a stage, as may be prescribed, while having adequate flexibility and academic freedom to explore, innovate and be creative and appropriately reflecting the geo-cultural and linguistic diversity of the country, within the broad policy guidelines and the National Curriculum Framework for School Education as approved by the Central Advisory Board of Education'.

What is also available for public reference is the recommendation of The Education Commission (1964-66) that clearly indicates the intent of The Commission to look at CSS as an effective instrument to build a society grounded on the principles of equality and social justice. For actualizing this, what is necessary is acceptance of the principle of 'Inclusion' and percolation of the same across all levels of society. Discourses on the principles of social inclusion and exclusion are integral to any debate and dialogue on the principles of justice and equality. Over time the element of 'Inclusion' has been incorporated into the mainstream discussion on Education Policy as well. Common ways of thinking about inclusion and exclusion are:

- *Inclusion as a Right*: Since the 1950s there has been increasing dissatisfaction, amongst educators in many countries, with the practice of 'special education' which separates so-called 'disabled' or 'different' children from the rest of society and educates them in different schools.

Special education is seen as simply reinforcing problematic inequalities and exclusion.

- *Inclusion as Effective*: This argues that inclusive schools are more cost-efficient, socially beneficial and educationally effective than segregated special schools. Proponents criticize 'special education' programmes as unsuccessful.
- *Inclusion as Political*: Marginalised groups, such as scheduled tribes or castes in India or indigenous peoples, view the inclusion of their special interests and needs within mainstream education as a political priority. Inclusion is a means to redress power imbalances and to secure a greater share of resources, representation and involvement in society.

Inclusion may also be looked at as:

- *A Philosophy:* Built on the belief that all people are equal and should be respected and valued, as an issue of basic human rights.
- *An 'Unending set of Processes'*: In which children and adults with 'disabilities' have the opportunity to participate fully in all community activities accessible to people who do not have disabilities.

Inclusive education means that all students in a school, regardless of their strengths or weaknesses in any area, become part of the school community. Inclusive Education is an education system that changes to fit the individual child that addresses all types of individual needs, not just disability and focuses in classroom management, capacity building of teachers and building conducive learning environment.

Philosophy of inclusion hinges on helping students and teachers become better members of a community by creating new visions for communities and for schools. Inclusion is about membership and belonging to a community. Inclusion is based on the belief that people/adults work in inclusive communities, work with people of different races, religions, aspirations, abilities. In the same vein, children of all ages should learn and grow in environments that resemble the environments that they will eventually work in. When good inclusion is in place, the child who needs the inclusion does not stand out.

Parallel to multiple connotations and interpretations of the principle of 'Inclusions' there are certain prominent concerns that can be identified. These are particularly relevant in the context of a variegated and diversified society like India and hence it warrants particular care and attention of policy-makers and policy advocates. One should remember that any attempt to 'include' necessarily involves some form of exclusion – hence it is imperative to plan out the management of potential exclusionary forces and outcomes in advance.

Generally it is observed that social policies thinking about inclusion and exclusion often operate with an over-simplified understanding of what 'normal' society is, in relation to which 'other' non-normal groups, communities and individuals are identified, positioned and the level of their inclusion or exclusion assessed. By viewing society as made up of collections of groups and communities, this way of thinking also tends to ignore the differences of individuals within each of those normal/non-normal groups. Furthermore, one of the main critiques of social exclusion is its 'one-size-fits-all' approach which assumes that social inequality can be overcome by providing the same opportunities equally for all citizens. While this would go a long way towards correcting historic imbalances and injustices, it is short-sighted. One size does not fit all simply because citizens are not all the same, neither are they located in identical and stable social, economic and political positions.

In India, as in most other countries, the term Inclusive Education is largely interpreted as generating special facilities and provisions for the education of the 'physically and mentally challenged children'. This understanding certainly brings to focus the special needs of challenged children and the need to define and carve out special systems for such children so that they are not excluded from education that all other 'non-challenged' children get access to. However, what this argument fails to highlight upon is the plight of the large segment of children from rural, indigenous and economically poor communities who are totally marginalised and excluded from the regular education system either because of inadequate access or inappropriate infrastructure or poor quality of curriculum and pedagogy.

The Action Plan for Inclusive Education of Children and Youth with Disabilities 2005 defines Inclusive Education as 'In its broadest and all encompassing meaning, inclusive education, as an approach, seeks to address the learning needs of all children, youth and adults with a specific focus on those who are vulnerable to marginalisation and exclusion. It implies all learners, young people – with or without disabilities being able to learn together through access to common pre-school provisions, schools and community educational setting with an appropriate network of support services. This is possible only in a flexible education system that assimilates the needs of a diverse range of learners and adapts itself to meet these needs. It aims at all stakeholders in the system (learners, parents, community, teachers, and administrators, policy-makers) to be comfortable with diversity and see it as a challenge rather than a problem.' However, while articulating the goals and strategies of the action plan, a clear emphasis is laid on children and youth with disabilities as defined under the Persons with Disability Act (1995) and the National Trust Act (1999).

Today policy-makers and policy advocates both agree that in the Indian context, 'Inclusive Education' has to go beyond the Salamanca Declaration (UNESCO 1994) to transcend the issue of disability. It must concern itself with all marginalised sections of society *viz*. Dalits, tribals and indigenous people, religious and linguistic minorities, child labour and of course, the physically and mentally disabled and particularly the girls in each of these categories, whom the school system tends to exclude in substantial proportions. Research has shown that Inclusive education results in improved social development and academic outcomes for all learners. It leads to the development of social skills and better social interactions because learners are exposed to real environment in which they have to interact with other learners each one having unique characteristics, interests and abilities. The non-disabled peers adopt positive attitudes and actions towards learners with disabilities as a result of studying together in an inclusive classroom. Thus, inclusive education lays the foundation to an inclusive society accepting, respecting and celebrating diversity.

Globally much research and deliberation has been happening on the issue of Inclusive Education. The Dakar Framework for Action adopted a *World Declaration on Education for All* (EFA) in 2000, which affirmed the notion of education as a fundamental right and established the new millennium goal to provide every girl and boy with primary school education by 2015. EFA also clearly identified Inclusive Education as one of the key strategies to address issues of marginalisation and exclusion. The fundamental principle of EFA is that all children should have the opportunity to learn. The fundamental principle of Inclusive Education is that all children should have the opportunity to learn together. Despite the common experience of economic pressures and constraints among countries of the North and South, the literature related to economic issues in Inclusive Education emphasises different aspects of economic reform.

The Framework of Action on Special needs Education, endorsed by the 300 participants representing 92 governments and 25 international organizations who met at Salamanca, Spain, clearly articulates the term 'special educational needs' refers to all those children and youth whose needs arise from disabilities or learning difficulties. Action Plan for Inclusive Education of Children and Youth with Disabilities, August 20, 2005.

Studies undertaken by countries of the North typically focus on national and municipal government funding formulas for allocation of public monies. In countries of the South, the literature on resource support for inclusive education services focuses instead on building the capacity of communities and parents as significant human resource inputs, and on non-governmental sources of funding. This literature also tends to be case-based on particular countries, regions or programmes, rather than large-scale, multi-national studies as in the North. Strategies for resourcing Inclusive Education in countries of the South are much more varied and broader in scope-characterised by a focus on linking and co-ordinating services with health sectors, universities, community based rehabilitation programmes and vocational training programmes, etc.

Some education of the differently abled experiences may be illustrated, in this context, with a view to exhibit the strategies adopted by grassroots interventions.

Prayas, Jaipur

Prayas – Vocational Institute for Mentally Handicapped, located at Jaipur, Rajasthan has been working to rehabilitate and socially mainstream children with special needs in the area of mental health. The basic objective of this organization is to integrate children with mental challenges into the mainstream by promoting the concept of 'Inclusive Education'. They also work for creating supportive political and social environment for children with mental challenges. The key intervention strategies adopted by Prayas include:

- *Preventive Approach*: Detection and investigation of cases of mental challenge, health and RCH disorders etc.
- *Promotional Approach:* Basic education, non-formal education and employment based training.
- *Advocacy:* Dialoguing with state and national governments on special needs of challenged children, networking among NGOs and policy level advocacy and mobilisation of community for wider sensitization.
- *Integration of Challenged Children in Mainstream Society*: The benefits derived include increased awareness and acceptance of challenged children both by their parents and larger community as also an increased sensitivity of normal children towards mentally challenged children.

Getting educated together under one roof has enabled an understanding about the special needs of mentally challenged children and accepting them as dignified human beings. This in turn enabled the retention of and increased learning abilities among the mentally challenged children.

Mon Foundation, Kolkata

The interventions of Mon Foundation aim at protecting and promoting child rights through mental health and life skills education, creating an environment sensitive to mental health and integrating mental health in the spectrum of disability and Inclusive Education. The intervention, having started with focus on research to understand the prevalence of mental health problems and having gone through a strategic shift, currently emphasises inclusion of non-school going children (*e.g.,* – children living in slums and on railway platforms), training of care givers for Children in Need of Care and Protection, advocacy with policy-makers and opinion leaders and further research into the area of mental health and Inclusive Education.

Mon Foundation believes that the term development does not mean only physical development. Development in this context should be interpreted in a broad sense, adding qualitative dimensions of mental, emotional, cognitive, social and cultural development.

Hence the focus on life skill education with a view to ensure fulfillment of Right to Life with Dignity for all. The advocacy efforts of Mon have helped in gaining recognition for the organization among State Government departments – The Board of Primary Education has incorporated the issues of mental health into their Teachers' training manual. The Board of Secondary Education has shown positive interest in including Life skills into the curriculum. The SCERT, the Department of Science and Technology, the Council for Higher Education etc have all shown interest and support for Mon's activities. However, globally still many countries feel the need to maintain some form of segregated provision – either special classes in regular schools or special schools. Further, in most countries, Inclusive Education programming is limited, but there is a definite trend toward increased Inclusive Education.

The fact that there is a dominant articulating principle of exclusion does not or should not undermine the prevalence of other levels of injustice. To do so would risk the introduction of further modes of exclusion through, for example, homogenisation of differences, or the dangerous ignorance of vested interests. An example of this can be seen in critiques of some forms of multicultural education in the ways in which they emphasise aspects of difference but in the last resort assert the legitimacy of a dominant cultural order. In these approaches, social exclusion initiatives operate around somewhat crude categorisations of various social groups in relation to power and access to goods and services. When thinking about social inclusion in education and developing policy to aid it, it is necessary to consider the highly complex ways in which race, class, gender and other categories intersect and inter-relate to produce unique individual and group experiences. Unless this exclusionary character of Indian education is challenged, both theoretically and in practice, by application of the principles of Inclusive Education, the Common School System would never become a reality.

Centrally Sponsored Scheme (CSS) of 'Inclusive Education of the Disabled at Secondary Stage (IEDSS)'

The National Policy on Education (NPE), 1986 and the Programme of Action (1992) gives the basic policy framework for education, emphasising on correcting the existing inequalities. It stresses on reducing dropout rates, improving learning achievements and expanding access to students who have not had an easy opportunity to be a part of the general system. The NPE, 1986 envisaged some measures for integrating of children with physical and mental handicap with the general community as equal partners, preparing them for their normal growth and development and enabling them to face life with courage and confidence.

India has also been a signatory to international declarations like the Salamanca Statement and Framework for Action on Special Needs Education (1994) and the Biwako Millennium Framework for Action (2002) and the UN Convention on the Rights of Persons with Disabilities, 2006 that emphasise the need for fundamental educational policy shifts to enable general schools to include children with disabilities.

The Centrally Sponsored Scheme of Integrated Education for the Disabled Children (revised 1992) is presently being implemented in States and UTs in over 90,000 schools benefiting over 2,00,000 children with disabilities. The scheme was introduced with a view to providing educational opportunities for children with disabilities in general schools, to facilitate their retention in the school system. It provides for facilities to students with disabilities including expenses on books and stationery, expenses on uniforms, transport allowance, reader allowance, escort allowance, hostel accommodation and actual cost of equipment. The scheme also supports the appointment of special teachers, provision for resource rooms and removal of architectural barriers in schools.

An important policy development after 1992 has been the enactment of Persons with Disabilities (Equal Opportunities, Protections of Rights and Full Participation) Act, 1995. Article 26(a) of the Act makes it a statutory responsibility on the part of Central, State and Local Governments to provide free education in an 'appropriate environment' for all children with disabilities up to the age of 18 years. Article 26(b) of the Act calls upon appropriate governments and local authorities to promote the integration of students with disabilities in normal schools. In addition, the Act stipulates that the appropriate Governments and the local authorities, inter alia, shall make schemes for varieties of educational initiatives and strategies.

The Centrally Sponsored Scheme of Sarva Shiksha Abhiyan (SSA) has set time-bound targets for the achievement of Universal Elementary Education (UEE) by 2010. With 'zero rejection' as its cornerstone, the programme provides support for the inclusion of children with disabilities in general schools at the elementary level. SSA has a provision for the inclusive education component @ Rs. 1200 per child with special needs per annum. Under the programme, over 20 lakh children with disabilities have been identified and over 15 lakh children with disabilities in the age group 6-14 years have been enrolled in general schools. The increase in enrolment at the elementary level is expected in the coming years to lead to a surge in the demand for secondary education. This will include children with disabilities.

The National Curriculum Framework on School Education (NCF - 2005) recommends making the curriculum flexible and appropriate to accommodate the diversity of school children including those with disability in both cognitive and non-cognitive areas.

The CABE committee report on the Universalisation of Secondary Education (June, 2005) recommends that the guiding principle of Universal Secondary Education should be Universal Access, Equality and Social Justice, Relevance and Development, and Structural and Curricular Considerations.

Education and the Common School System has recommended making the curriculum flexible and appropriate to accommodate the diversity of school children including those with disability in both cognitive and non-cognitive areas.

The National Action Plan for Inclusion in Education of Children and Youth with Disabilities (IECYD) developed by the MHRD (November - 2005) emphasises the inclusion of children and young persons with disability in all general educational settings from Early Childhood to Higher Education. The goal of the Action Plan is – "to ensure the inclusion of children and youth with disabilities in all available general educational settings, by providing them with a learning environment that is available, accessible, affordable and appropriate".

Currently accurate data are not available in respect of the exact number of children with disabilities transiting from the elementary to the secondary level. As per census 2001 about 2 per cent of the total population constitutes persons with disabilities. Projections relating to the number of children with disabilities entering the secondary level will need to be made therefore on certain key assumptions:

- Sufficient inputs and crucial necessary interventions would have been provided at the ECCE and Elementary level for children with disabilities to ensure their retention and achievement levels through classes which would prepare them adequately for entering the secondary sector.
- The secondary school system would adopt structural, curricular and pedagogical reforms that will extend the access of secondary education to this hitherto marginalised section of society and make their participation at this level genuinely inclusive.

Children with disabilities constitute one of the largest groups that are still outside the fold of the general education system. Under the existing IEDC Scheme it has not been possible to cover all disabled children primarily because implementation has been based on receipt of viable proposals from the implementing agencies. No conscious effort has been made to target all disabled children. As SSA supports inclusion of children with special needs at the early childhood education and elementary education level, it is desirable to introduce a scheme for the disabled children at secondary stage. The scheme for IEDSS is therefore envisaged to enable all children and young persons with disabilities to have access to secondary education and to improve their enrolment, retention and achievement in the general education system. Under the scheme every school is proposed to be made disabled-friendly.

Aims and Objectives

The Centrally Sponsored IEDSS Scheme aims to:

- Enable all students with disabilities completing eight years of elementary schooling an opportunity to complete four years of secondary schooling (classes IX to XII) in an inclusive and enabling environment.

- Provide educational opportunities and facilities to students with disabilities in the general education system at the secondary level (classes IX to XII).
- Support the training of general school teachers to meet the needs of children with disabilities at the secondary level.

The objectives of the scheme will be to ensure that:

- Every child with disability will be identified at the secondary level and his educational need assessed.
- Every student in need of aids and appliances, assistive devices, will be provided the same.
- All architectural barriers in schools are removed so that students with disability have access to classrooms, laboratories, libraries and toilets in the school.
- Each student with disability will be supplied learning material as per his/her requirement.
- All general school teachers at the secondary level will be provided basic training to teach students with disabilities within a period of three to five years.
- Students with disabilities will have access to support services like the appointment of special educators, establishment of resource rooms in every block .
- Model schools are set up in every state to develop good replicable practices in inclusive education.

Target Group

The scheme will cover all children of age 14+ passing out of elementary schools and studying in secondary stage in Government, local body and Government-aided schools, with one or more disabilities as defined under the Persons with Disabilities Act (1995) and the National Trust Act (1999) in the age group 14+ to 18+ (classes IX to XII), namely:

- Blindness.
- Low vision.
- Leprosy cured.
- Hearing impairment.

- Locomotor disabilities.
- Mental retardation.
- Mental Illness.
- Autism.
- Cerebral Palsy.

And may eventually cover *(i)* Speech impairment and *(ii)* Learning Disabilities, etc. Girls with disabilities will receive special focus and efforts would be made under the scheme to help them gain access to secondary schools, as also to information and guidance for developing their potential.

Type of Scheme

This is a centrally sponsored scheme under which the Central Government will assist the States/Union Territories and autonomous bodies of stature in the field of education in its implementation on the basis of the criteria laid down. Assistance for all the items covered in the scheme will be on 100 per cent basis but assistance for the programme would be subject to policy guidelines issued and initiatives to be taken by the appropriate government for implementing the educational provisions of the P.W.D. Act.

Components of the Scheme

It is proposed to provide for educational facilities under this scheme for all children with disabilities that are included in general schools at the secondary and senior secondary level (classes IX to XII).

The Scheme will include assistance for two kinds of components, *viz.*:

1. student-oriented components; and
2. other components (*e.g.*, those relating to infrastructure, teacher training, awareness generation, etc.)

For the first group of components, it is proposed to provide assistance to States/Union Territories/Autonomous bodies @ Rs. 3000/- per disabled child per annum for specified items, on the pattern of SSA which provides assistance @ Rs. 1200/- per disabled child per annum for the elementary level. (This rate was fixed in 2001-02). The State Government will provide a top up of Rs. 600/- per child per annum towards scholarship for each child. This amount of Rs. 3000/- per disabled child per annum may be spent on the following components:

(i) Identification and assessment of children with disabilities. The assessment team may include an interdisciplinary expert team of special educators, clinical psychologists, therapists, doctors and any other professional support based on the students' needs.

(ii) Provision of aids and appliances to all students with disabilities needing them, if these are not already being provided for through existing schemes like ADIP, State Schemes, voluntary organizations, Rotary clubs etc.

(iii) Access to learning material ensuring that each disabled student will have access to learning material as per his/her requirement like Braille textbooks, audiotapes, talking books etc., textbooks in large prints and any other material needed.

(iv) Provision of facilities like transport facilities, hostel facilities, scholarships, books, uniforms, assistive devices, support staff (readers, amanuensis).

(v) Stipend for Girl Students with Disabilities. Since Girl students with disabilities face discrimination, they, in addition to availing facilities under all schemes specially targeting girls' education, will be given a stipend @ Rs. 200 per month at the secondary level to encourage their participation up to senior secondary level.

(vi) *The use of ICT*: Access to technology is especially relevant for the disabled as it increases their access to a vast amount of information not otherwise available. Computers provided to students in secondary schools will also be made accessible to those with disabilities. The scheme will provide for the purchase of appropriate technology by way of special software such as Screen Reading software like JAWS, SAFA, etc., for the visually impaired and speech recognition software for the hearing

impaired to develop computer vocabulary for the hearing impaired and modified hardware like adapted keyboards.

(vii) *Development of Teaching Learning Material:* The scheme will cover the expenses incurred on organizing the mobilisation of such support as certified by the School Principal/Educational Administrators. Financial assistance under this scheme will be available for purchase/production of instructional materials for the disabled and also for purchase of equipment required therefore. Wherever necessary, the available material will be translated and produced in regional languages. The scheme will also support workshops for adaptation in the curricular content and development of supplementary material, self-learning material for teachers and students at the secondary level of school education.

(viii) External support from an interdisciplinary team of experts such as educational psychologists, speech and occupational therapists, physiotherapists, mobility instructors and medical experts has to be coordinated at the local level. Support can be made available at the cluster level and needs of children with disabilities in a cluster of schools may be addressed. The expenses incurred on mobilising such support in the form of TA/DA and consultancy fee will be covered under the scheme for children and young persons with disabilities at the secondary school level. Funds may be drawn from the child specific funds of Rs. 3000/- per child.

Costs of non-beneficiary-oriented components like teacher training, construction and equipping of resource rooms, creating model schools, research and monitoring, etc., will be covered separately. These components would be as follows:

(i) Removal of architectural barriers to ensure that students with disabilities have access to each classroom, laboratory, library and toilet in the school. A detailed manual laying out norms and guidelines for accessibility

required by different types of disability will be developed at the central level with the help of the Office Chief Commissioner of Persons with Disabilities (CCPD), and the Rehabilitation Council of India (RCI). The scheme will support development of the accessible physical environment in existing secondary school buildings.

(ii) *Training of Special/General School Teachers*: Special teachers to be trained through regular programmes run by the National Institutes/Apex Institutes of RCI or under any other programme of the States. There should be a component of in-service training for resource teachers to equip them with handling of other disability area. All general teachers at the secondary level will be trained in particular strategies like making educationally useful assessments, planning an individualised and need specific curriculum, teaching styles which include audiovisual aids, appropriate instructional strategies, etc.

(iii) *Orientation of Principals, Educational Administrators*: This training will include developing strategies for management of inclusive education. This will include teachers (both special and general), local educational administrators, Principals/Headmasters of Institutions, parents/guardians of the disabled children.

(iv) Strengthening of training institutions and assistance to existing organization/NGOs to develop teacher's training programme in inclusive schooling and for educational interventions for specific disabilities.

(v) Provision of resource rooms and equipment for the resource rooms in one school per block/urban cluster. Norms in terms of size, accessible features will be developed with the support of relevant agencies at the Central and State level.

(vi) *Appointment of Special Educators*: Support from special educators will differ at the secondary level from that at the elementary level. Special Educators will be appointed in the ratio 1:5. Ideally every school where disabled children are enrolled should have the services of at least

one special teacher. If the numbers of children are less, this teacher could also work for other schools in the cluster.

(vii) Development of some existing schools as Model Inclusive Schools so as to accelerate the process of education of children and youth with disabilities with initiatives from parents, teachers, community and respective governments. Norms will be developed at the central level with the help of relevant state and national level agencies, to provide the whole range of support for these schools. Funds for these will be charged towards the research component.

(viii) Administration, Research and Development, and Monitoring and Evaluation. These will form an integral part of the IEDSS Scheme. The State Government/NGOs/Autonomous bodies will have to formulate proposals for designing and developing new assistive devices, ICT technology, teaching aids, special teaching materials or such other items as are necessary to give a child with disability equal opportunities in education. Every year 5 per cent of the funds available at the Central level will be earmarked for administration, innovative and R and D projects and monitoring and evaluation.

(ix) Environment Building Programmes upto Rs. 10,000/- per programme at local level. The scheme will provide funds only in cases where there are no other provisions for the items under other schemes operative at State/Central level.

Other Support

At the secondary level, all children with disabilities included under the general education system may not require adaptations in the teaching learning process and evaluation procedures. However there may be some who would require some adaptations. The States/UTs/Autonomous bodies can take the support of special teachers, SCERTs, DIETs, Special Schools, Resource Centres, Non-Governmental Organizations, State Boards and any other community institutions available at the local level for this purpose.

Adaptations in Examination Procedures: Some children with disabilities may require some adaptations in the evaluation procedures according to their special needs. The existing evaluation procedures can be reviewed at the State level and modified accordingly.

Provision for alternative modes of examination for children and youth with disabilities should be considered and provided by the Boards of Examination. This is being visualised mainly as a process of issuing appropriate orders and notifications by the Boards concerned. Separate budget as such is not planned under the scheme.

Partnerships and Linkages

Linkages with the different Ministries/Organizations like Ministry of Social Justice and Empowerment, Government of India, Rehabilitation Council of India (RCI); National Trust etc., will help in creating convergence of resources and funds for addressing the needs of children with disabilities. Co-ordination Committees at various levels *i.e.* State, District and sub-district levels will help the planning and implementation of inclusive education at the secondary level. Formation of Parents/Guardians Groups at community/village level for sharing of information regarding benefits available from the scheme for their wards will be encouraged.

Regulations for Relaxation of Rules

State Governments/UT Administrations/Autonomous bodies/other implementing agencies will make provisions for relaxation of rules relating to admissions, minimum or maximum age limit for admission, promotion, examination procedure so as to facilitate in improving access of children with disabilities to education. At the Secondary level, young persons with disabilities beyond 18 years will be supported for a period upto 4 years to help them complete secondary schooling.

Implementing Agencies

The Scheme will be implemented by the Education Departments of State Governments/UT Administrations directly. The States/UTs may involve Non Governmental Organizations (NGOs) having experience in the field of education of the disabled in the implementation of the scheme. The Scheme could also be implemented by autonomous organizations of stature having experience in the field of education and/or rehabilitation of the disabled. There will be an inbuilt-flexibility in implementation strategies and practices, depending upon the contextual needs and the authority to interpret or reinterpret the provisions of the scheme will lie with the Secretary, School Education and Literacy, Government of India.

Monitoring and Evaluation

Appropriate structures will be established at the Central, State, District, and block and city level to ensure obtaining feedback from functionaries at different levels. The implementing agency should set up an Administrative Cell to implement, monitor and evaluate the programme. The existing Administrative Cell set up under the IEDC Scheme should serve the purpose. In States/UTs where the Administrative Cell has not been set up, the State Education Department will initiate action to set it up. The Cell will consist of Deputy Director (in the scale of pay applicable in the State Government), a Co-ordinator (who will be a psychologist) in the scale equable to University Lecturers), a Stenographer and an LDC in the pay scale applicable to such posts in the State Government/UT Administration.

At the national level, a comprehensive monitoring mechanism would be evolved in MHRD with involvement of National Apex level Institutes like the NCERT and/or NUEPA and/or reputed voluntary organizations and/or individual experts and/or autonomous bodies. Data on Enrollment and performance of children with disabilities at the secondary stage in proforma to be developed at the central level will need to be maintained by the states.

The State Governments will oversee the utilisation of money and collect the quantitative data, and prepare state specific report and forward it to the MHRD monitoring unit.

State appointed local monitoring agency/authority would follow the guidelines and use the common evaluation format. The monitoring arrangements will include both qualitative and quantitative data. In addition to monitoring, review exercises can be undertaken periodically. Parents and village education committees will be involved in the monitoring process especially for qualitative aspects in schools.

Collaborations with SCERTs, State and District Resource Centres, block, cluster level resources will be developed for this purpose. University Departments, IASEs and CTEs will be involved, wherever available and feasible. In all these endeavors, performance with regard to girls and members of SC/ST will be specially monitored. Both State and Central Government may engage outside agencies like Institutes and NGOs, which have experience in the field of education to evaluate the impact of the scheme. Such evaluation can be financed under the scheme. 5 per cent of the total budget will be earmarked towards administrative cost, research, monitoring and evaluation.

The Rehabilitation Council of India-RCI

The Rehabilitation Council of India (RCI) was set up as a registered society in 1986. On September, 1992 the RCI Act was encacted by Parliament and it became a Statutory on 22 June 1993. The Act was amended by Parliament in 2000 to make it more broadbased. The mandate given to RCI is to regulate and monitor services given to persons with disability, to standardise syllabi and to maintain a Central Rehabilitation Register of all qualified professionals and personnel working in the field of Rehabilitation and Special Education. The Act also prescribes punitive action against unqualified persons delivering services to persons with disability.

Objectives

- To regulate the training policies and programmes in the field of rehabilitation of persons with disabilities.
- To bring about standardisation of training courses for professionals dealing with persons with disabilities.

- To prescribe minimum standards of education and training of various categories of professionals/personnel dealing with people with disabilities.
- To regulate these standards in all training institutions uniformly throughout the country.
- To recognise institutions/organizations/universities running master's degree/bachelor's degree/P.G. Diploma/Diploma/Certificate courses in the field of rehabilitation of persons with disabilities.
- To recognise degree/diploma/certificate awarded by foreign universities/institutions on reciprocal basis.
- To promote research in Rehabilitation and Special Education.
- To maintain Central Rehabilitation Register for registration of professionals/personnel.
- To collect information on a regular basis on education and training in the field of rehabilitation of people with disabilities from institutions in India and abroad.
- To encourage continuing education in the field of rehabilitation and special education by way of collaboration with organizations working in the field of disability.
- To recognise Vocational Rehabilitation Centres as manpower development centres.
- To register vocational instructors and other personnel working in the Vocational Rehabilitation Centres.
- To recognise the national institutes and apex institutions on disability as manpower development centres.
- To register personnel working in national institutes and apex institutions on disability under the Ministry of Social Justice and Empowerment.

REFERENCES

1. A Compilation of Notes on Common School System by Prof. Anil Sadgopal Presented at the Meeting of CABE at New Delhi in July 2005.

2. CABE: Report on the Universalisation of Secondary Education (June, 2005).
3. http://rehabcouncil.nic.in/index.htm
4. http://www.education.nic.in/secedu/sec_iedc.asp
5. http://www.education.nic.in/secedu/sec_iedc.asp
6. http://www.google.co.in/search?hl=en&q=inclusive+education+issues+and+intervention&meta=cr%3DcountryIN&aq=f&oq=
7. http://www.ias.ac.in/academy/misc_docs/sci_eduinsa_ias.pdf
8. ID 21 – Communicating Development Research – Approaches to Inclusive Education.
9. Subhrajit Sinha, Development Support, CRY. *subhrajit.sinha@crymail.org*
10. Inclusive Education: Achieving Education For All by Including those with Disabilities and Special Education Needs – Prepared by Susan J. Peters for The Disability Group, The World Bank.

Right to Education Act (RTE) Act 2009

What is the Act About?

- Every child between the ages of 6 to 14 years has the right to free and compulsory education. This is stated as per the 86th Constitution Amendment Act added Article 21A. The right to education act seeks to give effect to this amendment.
- The government schools shall provide free education to all the children and the schools will be managed by school management committees (SMC). Private schools shall admit at least 25 per cent of the children in their schools without any fee.
- The National Commission for Elementary Education shall be constituted to monitor all aspects of elementary education including quality.

History of the Act

- *December 2002*: 86th Amendment Act (2002) via Article 21A (Part III) seeks to make free and compulsory education a Fundamental Right for all children in the age group 6-14 years.

- *October 2003*: A first draft of the legislation envisaged in the above Article, *viz.*, Free and Compulsory Education for Children Bill, 2003, was prepared and posted on this website in October, 2003, inviting comments and suggestions from the public at large.
- *2004*: Subsequently, taking into account the suggestions received on this draft, a revised draft of the Bill entitled Free and Compulsory Education Bill, 2004, was prepared and posted on the http://education.nic.in website.
- *June 2005*: The CABE (Central Advisory Board of Education) committee drafted the 'Right to Education' Bill and submitted to the Ministry of HRD. MHRD sent it to NAC where Mrs. Sonia Gandhi is the Chairperson. NAC sent the Bill to PM for his observation.
- *14th July 2006*: The finance committee and planning commission rejected the Bill citing the lack of funds and a Model bill was sent to states for the making necessary arrangements. (Post-86th amendment, States had already cited lack of funds at State level)
- *19th July 2006*: CACL, SAFE, NAFRE, CABE invited ILP and other organizations for a Planning meeting to discuss the impact of the Parliament action, initiate advocacy actions and set directions on what needs to be done at the district and village levels.

The Right to Education: Frequently asked Questions

(i) Why is the Act Significant and what does it Mean for India?

The passing of the Right of Children to Free and Compulsory Education (RTE) Act 2009 marks a historic moment for the children of India.

This Act serves as a building block to ensure that every child has his or her right (as an entitlement) to get a quality elementary education, and that the State, with the help of families and communities, fulfills this obligation.

Few countries in the world have such a national provision to ensure both free and child-centered, child-friendly education.

(ii) What is 'Free and Compulsory Elementary Education'?

All children between the ages of 6 and 14 shall have the right to free and compulsory elementary education at a neighborhood school.

There is no direct (school fees) or indirect cost (uniforms, text-books, mid-day meals, transportation) to be borne by the child or the parents to obtain elementary education. The government will provide schooling free-of-cost until a child's elementary education is completed.

(iii) What is the Role Envisaged for the Community and Parents to Ensure RTE?

The landmark passing of the Right of Children to Free and Compulsory Education (RTE) Act 2009 marks a historic moment for the children of India. For the first time in India's history, children will be guaranteed their right to quality elementary education by the state with the help of families and communities.

Few countries in the world have such a national provision to ensure child-centered, child-friendly education to help all children develop to their fullest potential. There were an estimated eight million six to 14 year-olds in India out-of-school in 2009. The world cannot reach its goal to have every child complete primary school by 2015 without India.

Schools shall constitute School Management Committees (SMCs) comprising local authority officials, parents, guardians and teachers. The SMCs shall form School Development Plans and monitor the utilisation of government grants and the whole school environment.

RTE also mandates the inclusion of 50 per cent women and parents of children from disadvantaged groups in SMCs. Such community participation will be crucial to ensuring a child friendly 'whole school' environment through separate toilet facilities for girls and boys and adequate attention to health, water, sanitation and hygiene issues.

(iv) How does RTE Promote Child-Friendly Schools?

All schools must comply with infrastructure and teacher norms for an effective learning environment. Two trained teachers will be provided for every sixty students at the primary level.

Teachers are required to attend school regularly and punctually, complete curriculum instruction, assess learning abilities and hold regular parent-teacher meetings. The number of teachers shall be based on the number of students rather than by grade.

The state shall ensure adequate support to teachers leading to improved learning outcomes of children. The community and civil society will have an important role to play in collaboration with the SMCs to ensure school quality with equity. The state will provide the policy framework and create an enabling environment to ensure RTE becomes a reality for every child.

(v) How will RTE be Financed and Implemented in India?

This Act serves as a building block to ensure that every child has his or her right (as an entitlement) to get a quality elementary education, and that the State, with the help of families and communities, fulfills this obligation.

Few countries in the world have such a national provision to ensure both free and child-centred, child-friendly education.

Central and state governments shall share financial responsibility for RTE. The central government shall prepare estimates of expenditures. State governments will be provided a percentage of these costs.

The central government may request the Finance Commission to consider providing additional resources to a state in order to carry out the provisions of RTE.

The state government shall be responsible for providing the remaining funds needed to implement. There will be a funding gap which needs to be supported by partners from civil society, development agencies, corporate organizations and citizens of the country.

(vi) What are the Key Issues for Achieving RTE?

The RTE Act will be in force from 1 April. Draft Model Rules have been shared with states, which are required to formulate their state rules and have them notified as early as possible.

RTE provides a ripe platform to reach the unreached, with specific provisions for disadvantaged groups, such as child labourers, migrant children, children with special needs, or those who have a "disadvantage owing to social, cultural economical, geographical, linguistic, gender or such other factor". RTE focuses on the quality of teaching and learning, which requires accelerated efforts and substantial reforms:

- Creative and sustained initiatives are crucial to train more than one million new and untrained teachers within the next five years and to reinforce the skills of in-service teachers to ensure child-friendly education.
- Families and communities also have a large role to play to ensure child-friendly education for each and every one of the estimated 190 million girls and boys in India who should be in elementary school today.
- Disparities must be eliminated to assure quality with equity. Investing in preschool is a key strategy in meeting goals.
- Bringing eight million out-of-school children into classes at the age appropriate level with the support to stay in school and succeed poses a major challenge necessitating flexible, innovative approaches.

(vii) What is the Mechanism Available if RTE is Violated?

The National Commission for the Protection of Child Rights shall review the safeguards for rights provided under this Act, investigate complaints and have the powers of a civil court in trying cases.

States should constitute a State Commission for the Protection of Child Rights (SCPCR) or the Right to Education Protection Authority (REPA) within six months of 1 April. Any person wishing to file a grievance must submit a written complaint to the local authority.

Appeals will be decided by the SCPCR/REPA. Prosecution of offences requires the sanction of an officer authorised by the appropriate government.

Substantial efforts are essential to eliminate disparities and ensure quality with equity. UNICEF will play an instrumental role in bringing together relevant stakeholders from government, civil society, teachers' organizations, media and the celebrity world.

UNICEF will mobilise partners to raise public awareness and provide a call to action. Policy and programme design/ implementation will focus on improving the access and quality education based on what works to improve results for children. UNICEF will also work with partners to strengthen national and state level monitoring bodies on RTE.

India Clears Right to Education Bill

Six years after an amendment was made in the Indian Constitution, the union cabinet cleared the Right to Education Bill. It is now soon to be tabled in Parliament for approval before it makes a fundamental right of every child to get free and compulsory education.

More than six decades after Independence, the Indian government has cleared the Right to Education Bill that makes free and compulsory education a fundamental right for all children between the ages of 6 and 14.

The Union Cabinet has cleared the long-pending Right to Education Bill, which promises free and compulsory education to every child. The move should provide a much needed boost to the country's education sector.

Key provisions of the Bill include: 25 per cent reservation in private schools for disadvantaged children from the neighborhood, at the entry level. The government will reimburse expenditure incurred by schools; no donation or capitation fee on admission; and no interviewing the child or parents as part of the screening process.

The Bill also prohibits physical punishment, expulsion or detention of a child and deployment of teachers for non-educational purposes other than census or election duty and disaster relief. Running a school without recognition will attract penal action.

Observing that it was an important promise to children, as education would become a fundamental right; India's Finance Minister P Chidambaram said that it would be the legally enforceable duty of the Centre and the states to provide free and compulsory education.

He added that the human resources ministry would release the text of the Bill after consulting the Election Commission, in view of assembly polls in some states.

The Group of Ministers (GoM) entrusted with the task of scrutinising the Bill cleared the draft legislation early this month without diluting its content, which includes the contentious provision of 25 per cent reservation in private schools at the entry level, for disadvantaged children in the neighborhood. Some see this as a way of getting the private sector to discharge the State's constitutional obligation.

The Right to Education Bill is the enabling legislation to notify the 86th constitutional amendment that gives every child between the age of six and 14 the right to free and compulsory education. But it has been 61 years in the making.

In 1937, when Mahatma Gandhi voiced the need for universal education he met with the same stonewalling about cost that dogs the issue today. The Constitution left it as a vague plea to the State to "endeavor to provide free and compulsory education to all children up to age 14", but access to elementary school still remains elusive today.

It was only in 2002 that education was made a fundamental right in the 86th amendment to the Constitution.

In 2004, the government in power, the NDA, drafted a Bill but lost the elections before it could be introduced. The present UPA's model Bill was then lobbed back and forth between the Centre and the states over the matter of funding and responsibility.

Critics of the Bill question the age provision. They say children below six years and above 14 should be included. Also, the government has not addressed the issue of shortage of teachers, low skill levels of many teachers, and lack of educational infrastructure in existing schools let alone the new ones that will have to be built and equipped.

The Bill had earlier faced resistance from the law and finance ministries on issues involving the states' financial contributions. The law ministry expected problems to arise from the 25 per cent reservation, while human resource development ministry estimates put the total cost at Rs. 55,000 crore every year.

The Planning Commission expressed its inability to fork out the money; the state governments said they were unwilling to supply even part of the funding. The Centre was thus forced to think of footing the entire bill itself.

The draft Bill aims to provide elementary schools in every neighbourhood within three years – though the word 'school' encompasses a whole spectrum of structures.

A set of minimum norms have been worked out as there's the usual barrier of paperwork in remote rural and poor urban areas. The State is also obliged to tide over any financial compulsions that may keep a child out of school.

"Laws and Bills don't make children go to school. Initially, there will be problems because while everyone must understand their social responsibility, what matters is whether the right children will have access to this programme. They say the fee component will be given by the government, but it's not fair to put that cost on others", says Lata Vaidyanthan, Principal, Modern School, Barakhamba Road, New Delhi.

Still, educationists who' ve rooted for the Bill argue that sharing social responsibility should be seen as a privilege, not a burden.

The Constitution (Eighty-sixth Amendment) Act, 2002 inserted Article 21-A in the Constitution of India to provide free and compulsory education of all children in the age group of six to fourteen years as a Fundamental Right in such a manner as the State may, by law, determine. The Right of Children to Free and Compulsory Education (RTE) Act, 2009, which represents the consequential legislation envisaged under Article 21-A, means that every child has a right to full time elementary education of satisfactory and equitable quality in a formal school which satisfies certain essential norms and standards.

Article 21-Aand the RTE Act came into effect on 1 April 2010. The title of the RTE Act incorporates the words 'free and compulsory'. 'Free education' means that no child, other than a child who has been admitted by his or her parents to a school which is not supported by the appropriate Government, shall be liable to pay any kind of fee or charges or expenses which may prevent him or her from pursuing and completing elementary education. 'Compulsory education' casts an obligation on the appropriate Government and local authorities to provide and ensure admission, attendance and completion of elementary education by all children in the 6-14 age group. With this, India has moved forward to a rights based framework that casts a legal obligation on the Central and State Governments to implement this fundamental child right as enshrined in the Article 21A of the Constitution, in accordance with the provisions of the RTE Act.

The RTE Act Provides for the;

(i) Right of children to free and compulsory education till completion of elementary education in a neighbourhood school.

(ii) It clarifies that 'compulsory education' means obligation of the appropriate government to provide free elementary education and ensure compulsory admission, attendance and completion of elementary education to every child in the six to fourteen age group. 'Free' means that no child shall be liable to pay any kind of fee or charges or expenses which may prevent him or her from pursuing and completing elementary education.

(iii) It makes provisions for a non-admitted child to be admitted to an age appropriate class.

(iv) It specifies the duties and responsibilities of appropriate Governments, local authority and parents in providing

free and compulsory education, and sharing of financial and other responsibilities between the Central and State Governments.

(v) It lays down the norms and standards relating inter alia to Pupil Teacher Ratios (PTRs), buildings and infrastructure, school-working days, teacher-working hours.

(vi) It provides for rational deployment of teachers by ensuring that the specified pupil teacher ratio is maintained for each school, rather than just as an average for the State or District or Block, thus ensuring that there is no urban-rural imbalance in teacher postings. It also provides for prohibition of deployment of teachers for non-educational work, other than decennial census, elections to local authority, state legislatures and parliament, and disaster relief.

(vii) It provides for appointment of appropriately trained teachers, *i.e.*, teachers with the requisite entry and academic qualifications.

(viii) It prohibits:

- *(a)* physical punishment and mental harassment;
- *(b)* screening procedures for admission of children;
- *(c)* capitation fee;
- *(d)* private tuition by teachers; and
- *(e)* running of schools without recognition.

(ix) It provides for development of curriculum in consonance with the values enshrined in the Constitution, and which would ensure the all-round development of the child, building on the child's knowledge, potentiality and talent and making the child free of fear, trauma and anxiety through a system of child friendly and child centered learning.

REFERENCES

1. http://mhrd.gov.in
2. www.indg.in/primary-education/policiesandschemes/right-to-education-bill

Inequality of Educational Opportunity in India

Changes Over Time and Across States

Between-group economic inequality is a common phenomenon in mutli-ethnic societies. Suchine qualities often reflect persistent differences in the capacity of individuals from different social groups to seize market opportunities, either due to discrimination or market constraints. A society with unequal opportunities is said to be characterised by a low degree of social mobility, in that individual's economic success/status is largely predictable in terms of family background such as caste and religion. This immobility leads to intergenerational persistence in poverty, with serious implications for the process of development. What is needed is to promote a distribution of human capital where schooling varies along with individual's level of effort instead of family background and other characteristics for which they cannot be held responsible (Roemer, 1998).

In recent years, attempts were made to measure equality of educational opportunity in terms of schooling mobility using comparable household data sets with information on individual's family background.

- *Two Studies*: Dahan and Gaviria (2002) and Behrman, Birdsall and Székely (2001); adopt a regression-model approach to measure schooling mobility using data on children's schooling from Latin America. Educational mobility in these studies is modelled in terms of inter-generational persistence in schooling.

- Similarly, Schütz, Ursprung and Wößmann (2008) use comparable data on students from the TIMSS survey and develop a regression-based index of the inequality of educational opportunity in 54 countries.

However, even if we focus exclusively on the instrumental value of education as productivity enhancer, inter-generational correlations serve as imperfect indices of the inequality of educational opportunity for at least two reasons. *Firstly*, they relate a limited set of circumstances beyond the individual's control (usually the father's or mother's value for a well-being outcome) to his/her well-being outcome. Thereby, by construction, attributing too much of welfare inequality to characteristics for which individuals should be held accountable. In the inequality of opportunity literature the idea is to account for as many circumstances beyond the individual's control as possible.

Secondly, consider the distributions of well-being conditioned by circumstances beyond individual's control. If their dissimilarities are deemed to contribute to inequality of opportunity then inter-generational correlations are inappropriate to measure inequality of opportunity even in hypothetical societies where just one single parental attribute constitutes the set of circumstances beyond the individual's control. As Yalonetzky (2009b) shows, several joint distributions of parental and offspring's well-being (*e.g.*, education) can produce the same inter-generational correlations. By contrast studies like Gasparini (2002), Checci and Peragine (2005), Lefranc *et al.* (2008), Ferreira and Gignoux (2008) and Barros *et al.* (2009) have developed and implemented indices of inequality of opportunity that handle multivariate sets of circumstances, which is a minimum methodological requirement for quantifying inequality of opportunity. In this study, we follow an approach similar to that of Ferreira and Gignoux (2008).

The key challenge in empirically assessing the degree of inequality of opportunity is to find dataon exogenous circumstance factor for adults and their parents. The most widely referred circumstance factor is parental education. However, no nationally representative large scale datasets for India provides this information for adults (*i.e.,* individuals for whom schooling data is not censored). In the absence of such data, our study focuses on two other commonly studied 'circumstance factors', namely, gender and religion of the individual. Using data on caste, gender and religion, the objective of this paper is to look at the interplay between social origins and gender in the determination of educational opportunity in contemporary India. The key questions that we address are:

(a) Are educational opportunities in India becoming more equal?

(b) Are there intra-and inter-regional disparities in educational opportunities?

(c) If so, how much mobility is there over time – do states that were less equal in the past have remained so today?

To explore the Indian experience of progress in equalising educational opportunities, we use National Sample Survey (NSS) data spanning the time period 1983-2004. We calculate three indices – a Pearson-Cramer (PC) index, an overlap index and a special Giniindex – in order to measure inequality of educational opportunity across Indian states. The PC index is related to one of Roemer's definitions of equality of opportunity. It takes the value of zero if and only if conditional distributions of well-being are identical across social groups and it takes its maximum value of one if and only if there is complete, or absolute, association between social group partitions and values of the outcome. We also estimate a multivariate, multiple group version of the overlap index originally proposed by Weitzman (1970). The overlap index is also equal to zero if and only if conditional distributions are identical across groups. Bothindices share the benchmark of perfect equality of opportunity. However while the PC index is sensitive to different group sizes, the overlap index compares 'representative agents' from each and every group independently of size. Therefore, with these indices, we offer results that are consistent with both approaches to group size. In addition, we estimate Lefranc *et al.*'s Gini of opportunity. It is an interesting index based on a definition of inequality of opportunity different to Roemer's. It measures Gini-inequality over Sen's welfare metric (1976) across social groups. Because the study is based on household datasets, we can describe the trends in inequality of opportunity between states and regions. In addition, we study exchange mobility of Indian states and regions in terms of decline in inequality of educational opportunity over time. Irrespective of the index used, the state of Kerala stands out as the least unequal in terms of educational opportunities. However, even after excluding Kerala, significant inter-state divergence persists amongst the remaining states. Transition matrix analysis confirms substantial exchange mobility in inequality of opportunity across India states. Rajasthan and Gujarat in the West and Uttar Pradesh and Bihar in the Centre experienced large falls in the ranking of inequality of opportunities. However, despite being home to a large number of poor people, Eastern states of West Bengal and Orissa made significant progress in reducing inequality of opportunity whilst the situation worsened in Bihar. At a region level, Southern, North-eastern and Eastern regions experienced upward mobility in terms of decline in inequality of opportunity, whereas the Central region experienced downward mobility.

The results show that India's record in reducing inequality of educational opportunity in post-liberalisation is characterised by considerable variation across states and regions. The state of Kerala stands out as the least unequal in terms of educational opportunities irrespective of the index used. In general, Southern states experienced lower inequality in educational opportunity when compared to Northern states. This finding is consistent with observed North-South divide in social outcomes in India – numerous earlier studies have pointed out how Southern states such as Kerala and Tamil Nadu differ from Uttar Pradesh and Bihar in education and health outcomes (Dyson and Moore, 1983; Dreze and Sen, 1995). In addition, even after excluding the single success story, Kerala, significant inter-state divergence remains amongst the remaining states. Our findings show that different kinds of problem arise in different parts of India. The incidence of rural poverty is high in the Eastern states of Bihar, Orissa, and West Bengal. Yet both West Bengal and Orissa made significant progress in reducing inequality of opportunity whilst the situation worsened in Bihar. On average, states with more accountable governments, greater access to finance, greater reduction in poverty, and greater inclusion of women in economic growth emerged as those that also succeeded in reducing inequality of educational opportunities. In other words, although not causal, significant positive associations were found between policy variables, poverty reduction, GDP growth elasticity of poverty, growth rates and reduction in inequality of educational opportunities. The policies we have identified may be reducing inequality of opportunity because they positively affect economic growth and enhance the poverty effect of such growth. Because the study period provides with both pre-and post-reform data on India, it is tempting to attribute the rising inequality of opportunities in some states and in some measures of opportunity to market reforms. The last decade has been a period of unprecedented improvement in living standards, thanks to liberalisation. The accelerated progress of elementary education in the nineties in some states may have been a response to weakening of credit constraints and increasing market returns to education which followed economic reforms and liberalisation of 1990s. Therefore the finding of a positive correlation between reduction of inequality of educational opportunity and poverty reduction and growth is reassuring. If true, this suggests that social inequality does not matter as long as economic growth and poverty reduction is in place. However, as argued by Dreze and Deaton (2002), "Much else than liberalisation has happened in the nineties, and while issues of economic reform are of course extremely important, so are other aspects of economic and social policy".

It will be interesting to follow up this study using more recent data in the near future. The last couple of years have seen marked improvement in school participation which is arguably due to the Sarva Shiksha Abhiyan (SSA) 'education for all' initiative. SSA aimed at achieving five years of primary schooling for all children by 2007. None the less, completion rates for grade had only reached 70 per cent by 2005-6 with significant variations across states. Similarly, although the SSA scheme aimed at achieving eight years of schooling for children aged 14-17 years, only slightly more than 50 per cent of all 15-year-olds had completed eight years of schooling in 2004. Eventhen, considerable cross-state differences remained (Dougherty and Herd, 2008). Moreover, attention needs to be given to circumstance factors such as childhood poverty that affect schooling directly and are common across some social groups.

REFERENCES

1. M. Niaz Asadullahand Gaston Yalonetzky. (August 2010). *Inequality of Educational Opportunity in India: Changes over Time and Across States*. Germany: IZA DP No. 5146.

The Role of Government of India in Education

One of the major educational controversies today refers to the role of the Government of India in education. *Prima facie* education is a State subject. Entry 11 of the List II of the Seventh Schedule to the Constitution lays down that "education including universities, subject to the provisions of Entries 63, 64, 65 and 66 of List I and Entry 25 of List III" should be a State subject. But there are some other provisions in the Constitution itself which contradict the almost absolute delegation of authority suggested by this entry in the State list; and what is even more significant, the Central Government has since shown an unprecedented activity and interest in the field of education ever since the attainment of independence. In 1947, it appointed a University Commission and has since been engaged in evolving common policies in Higher education such as the introduction of the three-year degree course. This was followed by a Secondary Education Commission which tried to introduce a number of uniform trends in a field where the Centre has had hardly any constitutional authority. No Commission was appointed in the field of Primary education. But the scheme of Basic education was declared to have gone beyond the stage of experimentation and was also adopted as the national pattern at the Elementary stage. The interest of the Central Government in Technical education and scientific research has been too obvious to need any illustration. Besides, an innumerable number of Committees and Reports have tried to iron out an all-India thought, policy and programme in almost every sector of education. Of still greater importance is the revival of the Central grants for education which had been discontinued in 1918-19.

In the period of post-war reconstruction as well as in the first and second Plans, substantial grants were given to the States towards the implementation of a large variety of educational programmes. With the adoption of the technique of Five-year Plans and the creation of the Planning Commission, the real authority to determine policies, priorities and programmes has now passed on from the States to the Centre in most sectors of development; and as a corollary to this major shift in all developmental activity, it is alleged that the, educational progress in the States is now more dependent upon the financial. The reactions at the Centre and in the States to these developments have been extremely divergent. On the one hand, the State Governments have grown more and more critical and resentful of this policy. They claim that Education is essentially their preserve; that they understand their educational needs much better than the Centre itself; and that the attempt of the Centre to cut into their sphere has generally done more harm than good to the cause of education. They also plead that Central grants should be placed at the disposal of the States without any strings attached and they are extremely critical of the manner in which their proposals are scrutinised, modified or amended by the Centre while grants are being sanctioned. On the other hand, the Centre also is not happy about the situation. It has assumed the role of dominant partner without having any constitutional authority to compel the States to conform to its dictates and without even having a machinery to report on the implementation of its programmes through the State Governments. Its main complaint is that its genuine desire to help the States is misunderstood as interference; that the reasonable minimum safe guards which are and should be adopted in all financial sanctions are misinterpreted as 'indirect pressures' or as 'leading strings'; that the States do not appreciate the larger interests of education underlying the policies and programmes proposed by it; that the States do not often implement the sanctioned schemes in the manner in which they ought to be implemented; and that it often finds itself helpless to enforce the directives given by it.

During the last ten years, therefore, education has developed practically into a 'joint responsibility' of the Central and State Governments. But unfortunately, neither partner is satisfied with the present position nor does each one of them have a number of charges to make against the other. It would be no exaggeration to say that it is this conflict and contradiction in the present position which is at the root of most of our administrative difficulties and it is for the solution of the set troubles that the role of the Government of India in education has to be properly defined as early as possible.

In order to pose correctly the complex problems involved in this issue and to arrive at some tentative solutions, it is necessary to consider the problem from three different points of view. The *first* approach would be historical and it would show how the role of the Government of India in education has varied from time to time and why; the *second* would start with the analysis of the relevant constitutional provisions and explain what the Constitution expects the Government of India to do in education; and the *third* would compare and contrast the role of the Government of India in education with that of some other federal governments in the world. It is only in the light of the findings of these three specific studies that it may finally be possible to draw up some kind of a picture of the role of the Government in education as it ought to be.

Historical Survey (1773-1950)

- *From 1773 to 1833:* The Government of India may be said to have been born with the Regulating Act of 1773 which designated the Governor in Council of Bengal as the Governor-General in Council of Bengal and gave him a limited authority over the Governors of Bombay and Madras. This authority was substantially increased by the Pitt's India Act of 1784. But prior to 1833, education in India had made but little progress (it has, in fact, been accepted as a State responsibility only as late as in 1813) and the Governor-General of Bengal did little to control or directs the educational policies of the other parts of India. At this time, therefore, 'education' may be said to have been a 'provincial' matter, subject only to the distant co-ordinating authority of the Court of Directors in England.

- *From 1833 to 1870*: The Charter Act of 1833 introduced a unitary system of Government. Under this arrangement, all revenues were raised in the name of the Central Government and all expenditure needed its approval. The Provincial Governments could not spend even one rupee or create a post, however small, without the approval of the Government of India which also was the only law-making body for the country as a whole. In other words, all executive, financial and legislative authority was exclusively vested in the Central Government and the Provinces merely acted as its agents.

As may easily be imagined, education thus became a purely 'Central' subject in 1833 and the entire authority in education and responsibility for it came to be vested in the Government of India. This excessively centralised system, which became more and more inconvenient as education began to expand and the territories of the Company began to grow, remained inforce till 1870. As administrative difficulties began to grow, some small powers were delegated to Provincial Governments from time to time and their proposals, as those of the 'authority on the spot', carried great weight. But the character of the system remained unaltered throughout the period and education continued to be a Central subject in every sense of the term.

- *From 1870 to 1921*: In 1870, however, Lord Mayo introduced a system of administrative decentralisation under which the Provincial Governments were made responsible for all Expenditure on certain services – inclusive of education – and were given, for that purpose, afixed grant-in-aid and certain sources of revenue. Education thus became a 'provincial subject' for purposes of day-to-day administration. But it has to be remembered that the Central Government still retained large powers of control over it. For instance, both the Central and Provincial Legislatures had concurrent powers to legislate on all educational matters. It was because of this concurrent legislative jurisdiction, that the Government of India could pass the Indian Universities Act in 1904 and could also legislate for the establishment of new universities. Of the new universities established during this period of British India, only one – Lucknow – was established by an Act of the U.P. Legislature. All others – Punjab (1882), Allahabad (1887), Banaras (1915), Patna (1917), Aligarh (1920) and Dacca (1920) were established by the Central Legislature. It was for the same reason that Gokhale could then introduce his Bill for compulsory Primary education in India in the Central legislature, although it failed to pass. In administrative matters, the sanction of the Government of India was needed to the creation of all new posts above a given salary and in 1897, the Indian Educational Service was created and placed in charge of all the important posts in the Provincial Education Departments.

In financial matters, the powers reserved to the Central Government were very wide. Its approval was required to all expenditure above a given figure and to the over-all budget of the Provinces. These large powers of control and supervision were justified on the ground that the Provincial Governments were responsible to the British Parliament through the Government of India. But whatever the cause, the net result of these powers was to make education not so much a 'provincial subject' as a 'concurrent subject' with two reservations: *(i)* the authority delegated to the Provincial Governments was fairly large; and *(ii)* the interest shown by the Government of India in education was very uneven and depended mostly upon the personalities of the Governor-Generals – a Ripon or a Curzon could make education look almost like a 'Central subject' while, at other times, it became almost a 'provincial subject'. It must also be noted that the interest and authority of the Government of India was not restricted to any particular field, although it naturally showed very great interest in University education. It appointed the Indian Universities Commission of 1917-19. As stated earlier it passed the Indian Universities Act in 1904 and also incorporated most of the new universities created in this field. It sanctioned large grants-in-aid for the improvement of Secondary and Primary education and for the introduction of science teaching. It also reviewed and laid down policies in such matters as the education of girls, or Anglo-Indians and the establishment of schools of art.

The Indian Education Commission of 1882 and the Government Resolutions on Educational Policy issued in 1904 and 1913 covered almost every aspect of education. In short, the view taken in this period was that education is a subject of national importance and that the Government of India must hold itself responsible for the formulation of over-all educational policy; and this view was particularly strengthened in the period between 1900 and 1921 because educational developments were intimately connected with the growth of nation; consciousness and the struggle for Independence. The main function of a federal government in education – to decide national policies in education – was thus clearly understood and accepted during this period.

The need of expert technical advice in education at the Government of India level was also felt during this period and the post of a Director-General of Education – who was to be an educationist and not a civilian and whose duty it was to advise the Government of India on educational matters

– was created by Lord Curzon and at the present time, when the very need of an advisory educational service at the Centre is being challenged in certain quarters, it may be well to recall Lord Curzon's defence of the creation of this post:

"My last topic is the desirability of creating a Director General of Education in India. Upon this point I will give my opinions for what they may be worth. To understand the case we must first realise what the existing system and its consequences are. Education is at present a sub-heading of the work of the Home Department, already greatly overstrained. When questions of supreme educational interests are referred to us for decision, we have no expert to guide us, no staff trained to the business, nothing but the precedents recorded in our files to fall back upon. In every other department of scientific knowledge – sanitation, hygiene, forestry, mineralogy, horse-breeding, explosives – the Government possesses expert advisers. In education, the most complex and most momentous of all we have none. We have to rely upon the opinions of officers who are constantly changing, and who may very likely never have had any experience of education in their lives. Under the system of decentralisation that has necessarily and, on the whole, rightly be pursued, we have little idea of what is happening in the provinces, until, once every five years, a gentleman comes round, writes for the Government of India the Quinquennial Review, makes all sorts discoveries of which we know nothing and discloses short-comings which in hot haste we then proceed tore dress. How and why this system-less system has been allowed to survive for all these years it passes my wit to determine. Now that we realise it, let us put an end to it forever. I do not desire Imperial Education Department, packed with pedagogues, and crysted with officialism. I do not advocate a Minister or Member of Council for Education. I do not want anything that will turn the Universities into a Department of the State, or fetter the Colleges or Schools with bureaucratic handcuffs.

But I do want someone at head quarters who will prevent the Government of India from going wrong, and who will help us to secure that community of principle and of aim without which go drifting about like a deserted bulk on chopping seas. I go further, and say that the appointment of such an officer, provided, that he be himself an expert and an enthusiast, will check the perils of narrowness and pedantry, while his custody of the leading principles of Indian Education will prevent those vagaries of policy and sharp revulsions of action which distract our administration without reforming it. He would not issue orders to the local governments; but he would be to advise the Government of India. Exactly the same want was felt in America, where decentralisation and devotion are even more keenly cherished, and had been carried to greater lengths, than here; and it was met by the creation of a Central Bureau of Education in 1867, which has since then done invaluable work in co-ordinating the heterogeneous application of common principles. It is for consideration whether such an official in India as I have suggested should, from time to time, summon a representative Committee or Conference, so as to keep in touch with the local jurisdictions, and to harmonise our policy as a whole".

The creation of this post, and the further creation of a separate Education Department in the Government of India in 1910 and the establishment of a Central Bureau of Education in 1915 made it possible to develop some other federal functions in education. For example, it is the duty of Government of India to collect educational data from the Provinces and to publish periodical reviewson the progress of education in the country – the *Clearing House function*. The Indian Education Commission (1882) recommended that the Central Government should bring out Quinquennial Reviews on the progress of education in India. Consequently, the first Quinquennial Review on the progress of education in India was published in 1886-87 and subsequent reviews were brought out in 1891-92, 1896-97, 1901-02, 1905-06, 1911-12,

1916-17 and 1921-22. Annual reviews of education were also published from 1913-14 onwards in all years in which the Quinquennial Reviews were not published.

Similarly, it is the duty of a Federal Government to carry out studies in educational problems (as part of its responsibility to provide leadership in educational thought) from time to time and to publish their findings. In particular, it is the responsibility of a Federal Government to study such educational developments in other countries as are likely to be of help in developing education at home. That both these responsibilities were understood accepted and even fulfilled with a great competence in certain areas, can be seen from the publications issued by the Government of India during this period. Moreover, 'the Government of India also published reports on important events of the period. In short, the research and publications function of the Federal Government was fully accepted and established during the period under review.

The co-ordinating function of a Federal Government was also recognised during this period. A reference to that has already been made in the speech of Lord Curzon quoted above. It was he who convened the first Conference of the Directors of Public Instruction in India at Shimla in 1901. Then started a regular practice of convening such Conferences for taking a periodical review of educational developments. An Educational Conference was held at Allahabad in 1911 and another Conference of the Directors of Public Instruction was held in 1917. With the passage of time, the need for such co-ordination was felt all the more keenly and a Central Advisory Board of Education was organized in 1920 with a view to assisting the Provincial Governments with expert advice.

Another function of a Federal Government to be recognised during this period was grant of financial assistance for educational development in the Provinces. Reference has already been made to the financial decentralisation introduced by Lord Mayo in 1870. That system continued to be in force up to 1876-77 when a system of 'shared revenues' was introduced. Under this system, certain revenues were exclusively designated as 'Central', certain others were designated as exclusively 'Provincial'; and the remainder was designated as 'Divided' and their receipts were shared between the Central and Provincial Governments according to an agreed contract which remained in force for a period of five years at a time. Thus the quinquennial contracts were revised in 1882-83, 1886-87, 1891-92 and 1896-97. In 1904, they were declared to be *quasi-permanent, i.e.,* not liable to be changed except in a grave emergency, and in 1912, they were declared as permanent. It will thus be seen that, under these financial arrangements, the entire expenditure on education was to be borne by the Provincial Governments within the resources allocated to them.

As may be easily imagined, these arrangements made the Provincial revenue fairly inelastic and they were unable to keep pace with the rapidly growing commitments of an expanding educational system. The Government of India, therefore, started the practice of giving grants-in-aid to Provincial Governments for educational development over and above the agreed contract arrangements. Thus the fifth important function of the Federal Government, *viz., financial assistance,* also came to be accepted during this period. Fortunately, the period between 1900 and 1921 was a period of boom in world finances and the Government of India had large surpluses in its budgets. It was, therefore, comparatively easy to allocate a share of these surpluses to the Provincial Governments for expenditure on education. The magnitude of these grants was fairly large and it may also be stated that most of them were specific purpose grants, *i.e.,* the Government of India decided the developmental policies to be adopted and earmarked the grants given for the implementation of specified approved policies. Only a few of these were general grants which were at the disposal of the Provincial Government were they free to spend in any manner they liked.

- *From 1921 to 1947:* Between 1870 and 1921, therefore, the day-to-day administration of education was delegated to the Provincial Governments and the Government of India continued to function as a Federal Government with five distinct functions, which came to be recognised, *viz.*, the functions of:
  - Policy-making.
  - Clearing house of information.
  - Research and publications.
  - Co-ordination.
  - Financial assistance.

With the coming into force of the Government of India Act, 1919, however, the position changed completely. The basic idea underlying this Act was that the Government of India should continue to be responsible to the Secretary of State for India that the functions of the Provincial Governments should be divided into two parts – the reserved part being responsible to the Government of India and the transfer being under the control of elected Ministers responsible to the Provincial Legislatures. As a corollary to this decision, it was also agreed that the Government of India have very little or no control over the transferred departments because the Ministers could not be simultaneously responsible to the Government of India as well as to their elected legislatures. These were basic political decisions and it was rather unfortunate that the division of authority in education between the Government of India and the Provincial Governments had to be made on these political considerations and no fundamental educational issues involved. One would have preferred that problems such as the following should have been raised and discussed on this occasion:

- To what extent is education a national problem?
- What should be the role of a Federal Government in education?
- What should be the relationship between the Government of India and provincial Governments in educational matters?

But, unfortunately, all such basic problems were ignored and the only questions discussed from a political angle were the following:

- Should education be a transferred subject or not?
- What should be the control which Government of India should have over education?

The Montagu-Chelmsford Report suggested that the 'guiding principle should be to include in the transferred list those departments which afford most opportunity for local knowledge and social service, those in which Indians have shown themselves to be keenly interested, those in which mistakes which may occur, though serious, would not be irremediable, and those which stand most in need of development.' In pursuance of this principle, it was but natural to expect that education would be classed as a transferred subject, although one does not feel very happy to be told that mistakes in education are not really very important. It was, therefore, decided that, excepting for the following few reservations, education should be a Provincial subject and transferred to the control of the Indian Ministers:

1. The Banaras Hindu University and such other new universities as may be declared to be all-India by the Governor-General-in-Council were excluded on the ground that these institutions were of an all-India character and had better be dealt with by the Government of India itself;
2. Colleges for Indian chiefs and educational institutions maintained by the Governor-General-in-Council for the benefit of members of His Majesty's Forces or other public servants, or their children were also excluded on the ground that these institution sought to be under the direct control of the Government of India.
3. The education of Anglo-Indians and Europeans was treated as a provincial but a reserved subject.

The authority to legislate on the following subjects was reserved for the Central legislature, mainly with a view to enabling the Government of India to take suitable action on the report of the Calcutta University Commission:

- Questions regarding the establishment, constitution and functions of new universities.
- Questions affecting the jurisdiction of any university outside its province.
- Questions regarding the Calcutta University and the reorganisation of Secondary education in Bengal (for a period of five years only after the introduction of the Reforms).

As a corollary to this decision, it was also decided that the Government of India should have no control over education in the Provinces.

Thus came about what the Hartog Committee has rightly described as the 'divorce' of the Government of India from education. As could easily be imagined, the results were far from happy. The Central interest in education disappeared almost completely after 1921; and when the need for retrenchment arose in 1923, the first victims were.

- Education Department of the Government of India which lost its independent existence and was amalgamated with other departments.
- Central Advisory Board of Education which was dissolved.
- Central Bureau of Education which was closed down.

The Central grants to the Provinces or educational development also disappeared, even the few powers of legislation reserved under the Act of 1919 were not exercised, and the Government of India did little beyond the clearing house function of publishing the annual and quinquennial reviews of the progress of education in India.

The Hartog Committee strongly criticised this unhappy position and said: "We are of opinion that the divorce of the Government of India from education has been unfortunate; and, holding as we do, that education is essentially a national service, we are of opinion that steps should be taken to consider anew the relation of the Central Government with this subject. We have suggested that the Government of India should serve as a centre of educational experience of the different provinces. But we regard the duties of the Central Government as going beyond that. We cannot accept the view that it should be entirely relieved of all responsibility for the attainment of universal primary education. It may be that some of the provinces, in spite of all efforts, will be unable to provide the funds necessary for that purpose, and the Government of India should, therefore, be constitutionally enabled to make good such financial deficiencies in the interests of India as a whole".

It is also interesting to know that, for some time after 1921, there was an outburst of strong provincial feelings and the divorce of the Government of India from education was even welcomed in some quarters. But it did not take the Provincial Governments long to realise that this was a mistake and that something had to be done to create a national agency and machinery for the development of education. It was, therefore, possible to revise the earlier decision and the Government of India revived the Central Advisory Board of Education in 1935; the Central Bureau of Education was also revived, on are commendation made by the Central Advisory Board of Education, in 1937; and finally the old Education Department was also revived as a Ministry of Education in 1946. The decisions of 1921 were, therefore, very largely undone by 1947.

Between 1935 and 1947, therefore, the role of the Government of India in education was again broadened and the several functions which had fallen into disuse between 1923 to 1935 were again resumed. For example, the co-ordinating function was resumed with great vigour and the Central Advisory Board of Education addressed itself to the study and discussion of almost every field of educational activity and finally prepared, and presented to the nation, a plan for the educational development in India during the next 40 years (1944). The publication function was also resumed and there constituted Central Bureau brought out a large number of publications on different aspects of the educational problem in India. The clearing house function was continued and its extent and efficiency were improved. The only functions developed in the earlier period and not resumed now were two – research and financial assistance. In spite of these limitations, however, the larger and more significant role that was now being played by the Government of India was appreciated all over the country; and the general feeling was that this role needed to be further strengthened and extended.

This brief historical survey of the role of the Government of India in education will show that it has passed through a number of stages. Prior to 1833, it had hardly any role to play; between 1833 and 1870, education was virtually a Central subject; between 1870 and 1921, the day-to-day administration was vested in Provincial Governments, but the Government of India discharged five distinct functions, *viz.*, the functions of policy-making, clearinghouse of information, research and publications, co-ordinationand financial assistance; between 1921 and 1935, the wheels of the clock were turned back and there was an almost total divorce between education and the Central Government; but fortunately, more progressive policies were adopted after 1935 and the Government of India began to play, once again, a larger and a more fruitful role in education.

REFERENCES

1. J. P. Naik., The *Role of Government of India in Education*. Government of India: Ministry of Education.

Education under the Constitution of India and in Actual Practice

Soon after the attainment of Independence, the problem of the role of the Government of India in Education came up for discussion again when the Constitution was being framed. The thinking of the framers of the Constitution on this subject seems to have been influenced by two main considerations:

- The general model adopted in the U.S.A.
- The recommendations of the Hartog Committee.

As in the U.S.A., therefore, a fundamental decision was taken to treat education as a State subject and also to vest the residuary powers in education in the State Governments by making a specific enumeration of powers reserved to the Government of India in this field. Entry 11 of List II of the Seventh Schedule to the Constitution, therefore, lays down that "education including universities, subject to the provisions of Entries 63, 64, 65 and 66 of List I and Entry 25 of List III" should be a State subject; and the entries which give authority to the Government of India in education were worded as follows:

List I – Union List

1. The institutions known at the commencement of this Constitution as the Banaras Hindu University, the Aligarh Muslim University and the Delhi University, and any other institution declared by Parliament by law to be an institution of national importance.
2. Institutions for scientific and technical education financed by the Government of India wholly or in part and declared by Parliament by law to be institutions of national importance.
3. Union agencies and institutions for –
   (a) professional, vocational or technical training, including the training of police officers; or
   (b) the promotion of special studies or research; or
   (c) scientific or technical assistance in the investigation or detection of crime.
4. Co-ordination and determination of standards in institutions for Higher education or research and scientific and technical institutions.

List III – Concurrent List

Vocational and technical training of labour.

In respect of Primary education, however, the Constitution has made an exception on the lines recommended by the Hartog Committee. The intimate relationship between the provision of a minimum of free and compulsory education for all children and the successful working of a democracy which the Constitution decided to create is obvious. The Constitution, therefore, makes the following provision as a directive principle of State policy under Part IV: "45. The State shall endeavour to provide within a period of ten years from the commencement of this Constitution, for free and compulsory education for all children until they complete the age of 14 years".

The expression 'State' which occurs in this article is defined in Article 12 to include "the Government and Parliament of India and the Government and the Legislature of each of the States and all local or other authorities within the territory of India or under the control of the Government of India". The Federal Government is, therefore, under a constitutional obligation to participate in the programme of providing free and compulsory education for all children until they complete the age of 14 years.

Similarly, the Constitution also makes it an obligatory responsibility of the Government of India to promote the educational interest of the weaker sections of the people and makes the following provision: "46. The State shall promote with special care the educational and economic interests of the weaker sections of the people, and, in particular, of the Scheduled Castes and the Scheduled Tribes, and shall protect them from social injustice and all forms of exploitation".

The expression 'weaker sections of the people', as used in this article, is general and is not restricted to the Scheduled Castes and the Scheduled Tribes only. For example, it will obviously include women and consequently the development of the education of girls and women becomes a special responsibility of the Government of India. In the same way, the expression also means people living in those areas where economic and cultural development lags behind. This article, therefore, makes it a responsibility of the Government of India to bring about an equalisation of educational opportunities in all parts of the country and, to that end, to give special assistance to the backward areas or States.

There is yet another provision in the Constitution which has an indirect but significant bearing upon the role of Government of India in education. Entry in the List III is 'Economic and Social Planning' and this implies that the Government of India has a constitutional responsibility for the economic and social development of the country as a whole. Now, it is a well-known sociological principle that economic and social development is intimately connected with education and it is in this sense that the White Paper on Education in the United Kingdom said: "Upon the education given to the children of this country, the future of this country depends". It is function of the schools to define the objectives of a national economic and social planning although they can, and should, to some extent, direct and influence their definition. But once the objectives of economic and social planning are decided upon by the powers that be, education has a very important role to play in assisting the nation to realise these objectives. For instance, the schools will never be able to decide whether democracy should or should not be a national way of life, whether socialism should or should not be accepted or whether rapid industrialisation should or should not be resorted to. But if the nation were to decide to accept these goals, education will help very greatly in creating and stabilising a social order based on these values by developing the necessary aptitudes, skills and interests in the rising generation. As Brubacher has observed, "schools can complete and consolidate a change decided elsewhere – whether by bullets or by ballots". The implication is obvious: an authority like the Government of India which is responsible for the economic and social planning of the country, cannot divest itself of a major responsibility in determining corresponding educational policies to realise its economic and social objectives.

In spite of the limited direct authority which the Constitution gives to the Government of India, therefore, practices have actually grown up, as a part of the formulation and implementation of the Five-year Plans of the country, under which the major educational policies are being decided; more at the Centre than in the States and the distribution of resources to education in general for the different sectors of education in particular, is becoming more a matter for a decision at the Central level than at the State levels.

On a very close examination of all the provisions of the Constitution which have a bearing on education, one cannot help the feeling that there is an element of basic contradiction in the role which the Constitution attempts to assign to the Government of India in education. On the one hand, the Constitution takes the simple stand that education, with all residuary powers, is a state subject except for a few special aspects specified within the Constitution itself. But the real trouble starts when the enumeration of these 'exceptions' begins. For instance, free and compulsory education is made an obvious exception on account of its cost and significance and Centre is given a specific responsibility for it (Art 45). Similarly, the responsibility of the Centre to equalise educational opportunities between different areas or different sections of society had also to be recognised and duly provided for (Art. 46). Then the responsibility of the Centre to safeguard the cultural interests of the minority and to see that they have adequate facilities to receive at least primary education through their own mother-tongue (Art. 350 A) as well as the special responsibility of the Centre to develop the national language (Art. 351) had also to be provided for. The need for controlled development of Higher education made it necessary to authorise the Centre to co-ordinate and determine standards in universities and scientific, technical, or research institutions (Entry 66 of List I) and, on account of such factors as high cost, difficulty of securing suitable personnel, the need to obtain foreign assistance, etc. Scientific research, technical education, and the higher types of professional and vocational education had also to be assigned to the Centre (Entries 64 and 65 of List I). Certain educational problems which have a large significance at present such as securing of foreign assistance (in men, materials or money) for education, training of Indians abroad, relationship with international organizations like UNESCO, participation in bilateral or multi-lateral programmes of educational assistance like the Commonwealth Co-operation Scheme or the T.C.M., had also to be left to the Centre under Entries 10 and 12 of List I. Finally, a very powerful means of central control was created when 'Economic and Social Planning' was made a concurrent responsibility (Entry 20 of List III).

These exceptions are so large that they circumscribe the State authority for education very materially and make education look more like a 'joint' responsibility than like a

State preserve. But this is not all. It has to be remembered that the Constitution was out to create a 'strong' Centre. It has, therefore, rested most of the important resources in the Government of India and the result is that no State has adequate resources of its own to develop education – the costliest of welfare services. Consequently the Centre, which controls the purse-strings, necessarily has the most dominating voice in the overall determination of policies, priorities and programmes. From this point of view, therefore, education begins to look, not only as a joint responsibility, but almost like a 'partnership' in which the Government of India plays the role of the 'Big Brother'. This implied constitutional role of the Government of India in education, therefore, is directly opposed to the explicit role as stated in Entry 11 of List II; and it is this basic contradiction inherent in the Constitutional provisions that leads to most of the controversies on the subject.

The situation is further complicated by another consideration. The role of a federal government in education is determined, not so much by the provisions of the Constitution as by conventions and practices evolved through historical developments. Perhaps the finest example of this is the Constitution of the U.S.A., itself. As is well-known, the tradition of local control in education is extremely strong in the U.S.A. and both in history and in law; education is specifically a State subject. The country has consequently developed a highly decentralised system of educational administration and it is worthy of note that the federal constitution does not even contain a reference to 'schools' or 'education'. All these factors should tend to make the role of the U.S., federal government in education extremely weak. But the facts are that federal aid to education is older than the federal constitution; and the present functions and responsibilities of the U.S., federal government in education are far heavier and more important than in several other countries where even the Constitution makes the federal government responsible for education in some way or the other. Today the U.S. Federal Government conducts a U.S. Office of Education which serves as a clearing house of ideas and information. It is also directly responsible for a number of educational programmes such as education for national defense (inclusive of the programme of the schooling of the veterans of the second World War), co-operation with other nations in a world-wide educational endeavour, in education in union territories and the education of the children of federal employees residing in government reservations, in dependencies and at foreign stations. Almost "every branch of the federal government conducts several educational activities... Congress has its Committees on education in both the House and the Senate.

The Supreme Court renders its interpretations in the form of decisions, as in the Dartmouth College Case, the MacCollum and Zorach decisions on public schools and religious instruction, the opinions on segregations in schools and colleges, and the interpretations on loyalty legislation affecting educators. Independent federal establishments that furnish educational service include the library of the Congress and its Copyright Office, the Government Printing Office, the Pan-American Union, the Smithsonian Institution, the National Museum, the National Gallery of Art, the National Academy of Sciences, the Commission of Fine Arts, the Atomic Energy Commission and the National Science Foundation. Much educational research is conducted in the Nation's Capital and sponsored by the Congress of the United States". In times of national crises, such as the depression of the 1930's, the federal government assisted a number of emergency programmes such as the Civilian Conservation Corps (CCC), National Youth Administration (NYA) Works Progress Administration (WPA), and other agencies. It has also assumed certain responsibilities for the education of backward groups like the Red Indians or Negroes. But above all, it has made large funds available for educational development without any idea of imposing federal control in education. As stated above, this tradition of federal financial assistance' without 'federal control' is very old and goes back to 1785 while the Constitution itself was ratified in 1788. The first grants to education were in terms of land, but very soon money grants were also introduced. The purposes for which federal grants were or are being given include:

- Agricultural education through the development of land-grant colleges with experimental farms and extension services attached.
- Vocational education in Secondary schools.
- Vocational training in distributed occupations.
- Vocational rehabilitation of the handicapped.
- Vocational guidance and placement etc.

All this, it must be said, is being done when the Constitution does not refer to education at all and the legal basis of all this huge and significant activity is the 'general welfare' clause in the Constitution. Hardly any other proof is needed to show that it is the historical background, and not the explicit provisions of the Constitution, that ordinarily determine the actual role of a federal government in education.

Assuming this thesis for the sake of argument, the relevant question is: what have been the developments in Indian education since the adoption of the Constitution and how have they affected the constitutional roles of the Government of India and the State Governments in defining and implementing educational policies? In this context, attention may be specially invited to three significant developments. The first is the growing desire to evolve a national system of education for the country as a whole. This desire found an expression as early as 1906 when the Surat Congress passed a resolution on national education. It was given a great fillip by Mahatma Gandhi in his Non-Co-operation Movement of 1921. But at this time, the idea was mainly restricted to few non-official agencies. When the popular Ministries came to power in 1937, the movement also assumed an official form and an attempt was now made to reorient all educational institutions to the concept of national education. This desire naturally became even stronger when popular Governments came to power both in the Centre and the States.

Such a desire obviously implies the assumption of a leading role in the formulation and implementation of educational programmes by the Government of India. The same implication has been further strengthened by the growing realisation of the fact that education has a national significance, that it would be almost fatal to the future of the nation to treat it as purely local, that a group of States each of whom is sovereign to decide its own educational policies may even do more harm than good to national solidarity, and that a Central agency to co-ordinate and develop a national system of education is inevitable in the present conditions when education is generally backward in all parts of the country and very unevenly developed in its different parts. It is this realisation of the national significance of education and the growing desire to create a national system of education that have led to the unprecedented activity of the Government of India in education during the last ten years and, to that extent, diminished the constitutional responsibility of the States for education.

A second development of the period which has also helped to give the Government of India a dominant voice in the formulation of educational policies is the revival of central grants for education to which a reference has already been made. This revival was of course inevitable in the financial and administrative set-up created by the constitution which vests all the best resources in the Centre and makes the States responsible for all the expensive social services. If the surplus resources at the Centre could have been passed to the needy States with little or no controls, the responsibility of the States for the development of education would have been strengthened. But this did not happen. The attempts of the Centre in policy-making often got mixed up with its attempts at financial assistance and thus arouse the charge that Central grants are being used as levers to secure acceptance of Central educational policies. That this charge is largely unfounded will be shown later; but one result of the large Central grants for education has to be admitted: they created a situation in which a very large part of the funds needed for educational development came from the Centre through grant-in-aid. Consequently, the States have tended to lose their spirit of self-reliance and self-confidence and are developing a habit of looking up to Delhi for almost everything.

The third development of this period which undermined the responsibility of the States for education and this was a development which has done the greatest damage in this sector – came from outside the educational field, *viz.*, the adoption of centralised planning and the creation of the Planning Commission. In the new technique of planning that has now been adopted, more and more decisions tend to be taken at the Centre than in the States. The decision on national targets, the fixation of priorities, the allocation of resources to different sectors of development or even to different programmes within the same sector of development, the allocation of resources to different States, the fixation of the Central assistance to each State – these and such other problems are mainly decided by the Planning Commission and all these affect educational policies so largely that a State Government is very often required, not to prepare an educational plan, but to fill in the blanks or details of a structure whose broad irrevocable outline has already been decided elsewhere. Even the Ministry of Education finds itself in the same weak predicament as the States *vis-a-vis* the Planning Commission. It is these developments that have contributed most to the trend to centralisation in education during the last ten years and it is because of them that the responsibility of States for education has been most weakened.

It will thus be seen that the inherent contradiction in the constitutional position has been still further accentuated by the developments of the last ten years and the role of the Centre has now become far more important in actual practice than in the cold print of the Constitution. It must also be remembered that these developments are not necessarily deplored. They are, in fact, welcomed in several quarters and today, a strong section of opinion in the country favours a proposal to amend the Constitution and to make education a concurrent subject. The lack of adequate leadership which is sometimes conspicuous at the State level and the frequently noticed distortion of State educational policies under immediately political or parochial pressures also tend to emphasise and strengthen this viewpoint. This equivocal position has given rise to a bitter controversy regarding the correct role of the federal government in education; and as suggested in the opening paragraphs, this problem will have to be satisfactorily solved at an early date.

REFERENCE

1. J. P. Naik., *The Role of Government of India in Education*. Government of India: Ministry of Education.

Quality Enhancement Programmes on School Education in India

District Primary Education Programme

The Centrally Sponsored Scheme of District Primary Education Programme (DPEP) was launched in 1994 as a major initiative to revitalise the primary education system and to achieve the objective of universalisation of primary education. Under the Programme parameters, investment per district is limited to Rs. 40 crore over a project period of 5-7 years. There is a ceiling of 33.3 per cent on civil works component and 6 per cent on management cost. The remaining amount is required to be spent on quality improvement activities.

DPEP is an externally aided project. 85 per cent of the project cost is met by the Central Government and the remaining 15 per cent is shared by the concerned State Government. The Central Government share is resourced through external assistance. At present external assistance of about Rs. 6,938 crore composing Rs. 5, 137 as credit from IDA and Rs. 1, 801 crore as grant from EC/DFID/UNICEF/ Netherlands has been tied-up for DPEP.

Major Achievements of DPEP

1. DPEP has so far opened more than 1, 60,000 new schools, including almost 84,000 alternative schooling (AS)

centres. The AS centres cover nearly 3.5 million children, while another two lakh children are covered by Bridge Courses of different types.

2. The school infrastructure created under DPEP has been remarkable. Works either complete or in progress include 52758 school buildings, 58,604 additional classrooms, 16,619 resource centres, 29,307 repair works, 64,592 toilets, and 24,909 drinking water facilities.
3. The Gross Enrolment Ratio (GER) for Phase-I states was around 93 to 95 per cent for the last three years. After the adjustment for the Alternative Schools/Education Guarantee Centres enrolment, the GER in the 2001-02 works out above 100 per cent. In the districts covered under subsequent phases of DPEP, the GER including enrolment of AS/EGS was above 85 per cent.
4. The enrolment of girls has shown significant improvement. In DPEP-I districts, the share of girls enrolment in relation to total enrolment has increased from 48 per cent to 49 per cent, while this increase in the subsequent phases of DPEP districts has been from 46 per cent to 47 per cent.
5. The total number of differently bled children enrolled is now more than 4,20,203 which represents almost 76 per cent of the nearly 5,53,844 differently-abled children identified in the DPEP States.
6. Village Education Committees/School Management Committees have been setup in almost all project villages/habitations/schools.
7. About 1,77,000 teachers, including Para-teachers/Shiksha Karmis have been appointed.
8. About 3,380 resource centres at block level and 29,725 centres at cluster level have been set-up for providing academic support and teacher training facilities.

Sarva Shiksha Abhiyan (SSA)

The '*Sarva Shiksha Abhiyan*' (Hindi: The '*Education for All*' Movement), is a flagship programme of the Government of India pioneered by Atal Bihari Vajpayee, Ex. Prime minister of India for achievement of universalisation of elementary education in a time bound manner, as mandated by the 86th amendment to the Constitution of India making free and compulsory education to children of ages 6-14 (estimated to be 205 million in number in 2001) a fundamental right. The programme aims to achieve the goal of universalisation of elementary education of satisfactory quality by 2010. There are 8 main programmes in SSA. It includes ICDS, Anganwadi etc. It also Includes KGBVY. Kasturba Gandhi Balika Vidalaya Yojana was started in 2004 with a view to give primary education to all girls.

Goals

- All in school by 2005.
- Complete 5 years of primary education by 2005 and 8 years of schooling by 2010.
- Satisfactory Quality with emphasis on education for life.
- Bridge all gender and social gaps at primary level by 2007 and elementary level by 2010.
- Universal retention by 2010.

Background

Constitutional, legal and national statements for universalisation of elementary education

1. *Constitutional Mandate, 1950:* The Directive Principles of State Policies postulates "The State shall endeavor to provide, within a period of ten years from the commencement of this Constitution, for free and compulsory education to all children until they complete the age of 14 years".
2. *National Policy of Education, 1987:* "It shall be ensured that free and compulsory education of satisfactory quality is provided to all children up to 14 years of age before we enter the twenty first century".
3. *Unnikrishnan Judgement, 1994:* "Every child/citizen of this country has a right to free education until he completes the age of fourteen years". Due to low attendance mid day meal was introduced.

Objectives

- All children in school, Education Guarantee Centre or Alternate School by 2003.
- All children complete five years of primary schooling by 2007.
- All children complete eight years of schooling by 2010.
- Focus on elementary education of satisfactory quality with emphasis on education for life.
- Bridge all gender and social category gaps at primary stage by 2007 and at elementary education level by 2010.

Interventions

There are fifteen interventions in SSA

1. BRC (Block Resource Centre).
2. CRC (Cluster Resource Centre).
3. *MGLC and AIE:* Alternative and innovative education (AIE) is one of the major interventions of SSA to provide access for all children to primary education. Various strategies have been developed for ensuring participation of children of marginalised and deprived groups in tribal and coastal areas.
4. *Civil Works:* The civil works component is important under SSA. Under this component, there is massive investment up to the limit of 33 per cent of the total project budget. Provision of school infrastructure helps in providing access to children, and also helps in their retention, both of which are important objectives of the SSA. Provision of infrastructure for Resources Centres at sub-district levels helps in creating academic support, which acts as a catalyst towards quality improvement. The following constructions are under taken under civil works.
5. Free text-books.
6. *Innovative Activities*: The innovative programmes implemented in schools are acting as a catalyst in the process of achieving useful and relevant elementary

education for all children in the 6-14 age groups and to bridge social, regional and gender gaps in the active participation of the community. The programmes are successful in creating interest in students on education and helped to retain their studies. The schemes implemented under Innovative Schemes are: Early Childhood Care and Education, Girls Education, SC/ST Education and Computer Education.

7. IEDC.
8. Management and MIS.
9. *R&E (Research and Evaluation)*: This intervention consists of Research, Evaluation, Supervision and Monitoring. The norms propose an amount of Rs. 1,500/- per school for the development of capacities and supervision through resource/research institutions on an effective EMIS. There are provisions for regular school mapping/ micro planning for updating of household data. The funds can be utilised for both government and government aided schools. Following activities are proposed under the intervention.
   (i) creating a pool of resource persons for effective field based monitoring;
   (ii) providing regular generation of community based data;
   (iii) conducting achievement test, evaluation studies;
   (iv) undertaking research activities;
   (v) setting up special task force for low female literacy districts and for special monitoring of girls, SC, ST etc.
   (vi) incurring expenditure on Education Management Information System;
   (vii) undertaking contingent expenditure like charts, posters, sketch pen, OHP pen etc., for visual monitoring systems;
   (viii) conduct cohort studies.

10. *School Grant:* School grant at Rs. 2, 000 each was given to schools under the project. Out of the school grant Rs. 1000 was given to improvement of school library facilities. The rest was utilised towards making the non-functional equipment functional, school beautification, repair and maintenance of furniture, musical instruments and over all environment development of schools.
11. *Teacher Grant*: In order to improve the class room transactions and preparation of teaching aids grant at Rs. 500 is given to all LP/UP teachers. The teachers utilised the grant to produce and procure TLM for effective classroom transactions. During 2007-08, 547590 teachers both LP/UP were benefited.
12. *Teacher Training*: The quality education is the most important goal of SSA. The various strategies to improve the training are:
    - *(i)* training and retraining of teachers;
    - *(ii)* familiarisation training on new curriculum and text books;
    - *(iii)* familiarisation training on National Curriculum Frame Work (NCF 2005);
    - *(iv)* Examination reforms;
    - *(v)* training on grading system and assessment on the impact of grading system;
    - *(vi)* scholastic and non-Scholastic areas improvement;
    - *(vii)* training of teachers on Inclusive Education for children with special needs
    - *(viii)* planning and implementation of quality education measures;
    - *(ix)* resource groups are strengthened at all levels (separate Resource Groups for each subjects) 300-350 Resource Person per district).

Follow up activities, on-site support and review meetings are ensured. DIETs identified training needs – hard spots and develop training modules. This process helped to improve the quality of training. Training for Trainers and Block Programme Officers was conducted.

13. Remedial teaching.
14. Community mobilisation.
15. *Distance Education:* The Distance Education Programme (DEP) is a National component of SSA, which is sponsored by Ministry of Human Resource Development, Government of India. It is being implemented by Indira Gandhi National Open University (IGNOU) in collaboration with all States/Union Territories of India. The DEP-SSA will be an important input in the in-service education of teachers and other personnel in the area of elementary education. It will supplement the face-to-face training by using Multi-media packages like audio-video programmes, radio broadcast, teleconferencing etc. The Distance mode of training would not only help address a larger number of individuals, but also would provide uniformity in training inputs and reduce the transmission loss, which is generally experienced in the face-to-face cascade model of training.

Activities

- Civil infrastructure developments and improving.
- Teacher training.

Achievements

This programme made significant achievements at village levels. In 2004 many villages in India were covered and preliminary education centres opened. In the south Indian state of Tamil Nadu, a village called Sattanathapuram (Town: Sirkazhi) located in Nagapattinam district, is one of the first village to implement this programme successfully. Afternoon meal schemes for poor kids in support of state government combined with education for all programmes made significant progress in literacy rate. Non-governmental organizations donated generously the lands for poor people and the construction of schools completed by Village Panchayats.

Rashtriya Madhyamik Shiksha Abhiyan (RMSA)

Rashtriya Madhyamik Shiksha Abhiyan (RSMA) is aimed at expanding and improving the standards of secondary education – classes VIII to X. The RSMA would also take secondary education to every corner of the country by ensuring a secondary school (up to class X) within a radius of 5 km for every neighbourhood. Rashtriya Madhyamik Shiksha Abhiyan (RMSA) which is the most recent initiative of Government of India to achieve the goal of universalisation of secondary education (USE).

The Sarva Shiksha Abhiyaan programme set-up by the government to bring elementary education to millions of children has been successful to a large extent, and has thus created a need for strengthening secondary education infrastructure across the country. The HRD Ministry has taken note of this, and now plans to implement a secondary education scheme called Rashtriya Madhyamik Shiksha Abhiyaan (RMSA) during the 11th plan at a total cost of Rs. 20,120 crore. "With the successful implementation of the Sarva Shiksha Abhiyan, a large number of students are passing out from upper primary classes creating a huge demand for secondary education", the HRD Ministry said.

Vision

The vision for secondary education is to make good quality education available, accessible and affordable to all young persons in the age group of 14-18 years. With this vision in mind, the following is to be achieved:

- To provide a secondary school within a reasonable distance of any habitation, which should be 5 km for secondary schools and 7-10 km for higher secondary schools.
- Ensure universal access of secondary education by 2017 (GER of 100%).
- Universal retention by 2020.
- Providing access to secondary education with special references to economically weaker sections of the society, the educationally backward, the girls and the disabled children residing in rural areas and other marginalised categories like SC, ST, OBC and Educationally Backward Minorities (EBM).

Goal and Objectives

In order to meet the challenge of Universalisation of Secondary Education (USE), there is a need for a paradigm shift in the conceptual design of secondary education. The guiding principles in this regard are; Universal Access, Equality and Social Justice, Relevance and Development and Curricular and Structural Aspects. Universalisation of Secondary Education gives opportunity, to move towards equity. The concept of 'common school' will be encouraged. If these values are to be established in the system, all types of schools, including unaided private schools will also contribute towards Universalisation of Secondary Education (USE) by ensuring adequate enrolments for the children from under privileged society and the children Below Poverty Line (BPL) families.

Main Objectives

- To ensure that all secondary schools have physical facilities, staffs and supplies at least according to the prescribed standards through financial support in case of Government/Local Body and Government aided schools, and appropriate regulatory mechanism in the case of other schools.
- To improve access to secondary schooling to all young persons according to norms – through proximate location (say, Secondary Schools within 5 km, and Higher Secondary Schools within 7-10 kms)/efficient and safe transport arrangements/residential facilities, depending on local circumstances including open schooling. However in hilly and difficult areas, these norms can be relaxed. Preferably residential schools may be set-up in such areas.
- To ensure that no child is deprived of secondary education of satisfactory quality due to gender, socio-economic, disability and other barriers.
- To improve quality of secondary education resulting in enhanced intellectual, social and cultural learning.

- To ensure that all students pursuing secondary education receive education of good quality.
- Achievement of the above objectives would also, inter-alia, signify substantial progress in the direction of the Common School System.

REFERENCE

1. Thamarasssrei, Ismail (2008), *Education in the Emerging Indian Society*, New Delhi: Kanishka Publishers.

Education of National Integration

National integration is national unity. It is unity in diversity. It means unifying all the forces in the country so as to give the idea of one nation. The problem national integration is very complex. On achieving independence we become pledged to built India in to a secular, democratic, republic based on the principles of social and economic justice.

In spite of our best efforts made in this sphere, India is still faced with many disintegrating. The foundation of our national life is common citizenship, unity in diversity, freedom of religion, secularism, equality, justice and fraternity among all communities. This foundation can be laid through education.

"India is my country; all Indians are my brothers and sisters. I love my country, and I am proud of its rich and varied heritage. I shall always strive to be worthy of it. I shall give my parents, teachers and all elders respect and treat every one with courtesy. To my country and my people, I pledge my devotion. In their well-being and prosperity alone lies my happiness". The echo of our unity is blowing in the pledge. A nation is said to be integrated if its citizens, may be belonging to any caste, community, religion, language and state have a feeling of oneness, share each others joy and sorrows, smiles and tears and have an interest in the welfare of the nation as a whole.

The citizens of an integral/integrated nation must have, mutual understanding, tolerance, respect for the culture, traditions, ways of life, common national ideas, common objectives, common interest, above all a, profound confidence in the future of the nation.

National Integration Involves

- The sentiments of nationalism.
- The feeling of oneness.
- Unity-especially unity in social, political, economic, emotional, linguistic, and cultural fields.
- Common ideals of life, common code of behaviour.
- The ability to subordinate sectarian and parochial loyalties to loyalty of the nation.

Need for National Integration

National integration is vital for India's survival at a time of when the country under the threat of foreign aggression as well as the internal centrifugal forces of:

- regionalism;
- communalism;
- linguism;
- racialism; and
- ethnicity.

It is necessary to meet the challenge of the present times.

Emotional Integration and National Integration

National Integration is the end where as emotional integration is the means to achieve the end. The basis of national integration is emotional integration. It is through training of mind and heart that a sense of oneness among the people of the country can be inspired. Emotional integration in this particular sense means a feeling of national pride and faith in the nation's greatness. When the emotions are conditioned by the idea of national loyalty and directed towards national welfare, the result is national integration.

Education can play a significant role on promoting national integration. The national unity was most conspicuous during pre-independence days. When the whole nation stood united to over-throw the foreign yoke and also when the security of the Indian boarders was threatened by Pakistan and China. But, in recent years there has been general weakening of this unity. Definite steps have to be taken to promote national unity. Education can play a very significant role here.

Hurdles in the way of National Integration

- Communalism.
- Casteism.
- Religious Prejudices.
- Provincialism.
- Regionalism.
- Linguism.
- Economic Imbalances.

Educational and National Integration

Dr. S. Radhakrishnan's Observes;

"National integration cannot be built by brick and mortar or with chisel or hammer. It has to growth silently in the minds of hearts of man by process by which it can be achieved is education".

A Matter of Feeling and Attitude

National integration is a matter of feelings; it is matter of attitude with the individual. Feelings and attitudes developed during the impressionable period, (usually school life) of ones life, continue to influence his life up to the last breath.

- *Muthaliar Commission;* "If education doesn't strengthen the forces of national cohesion and solidarity we are afraid that out freedom, our national unity as well as our (culture) future progress will be seriously imperiled".

National Integration through Education

Education can definitely play a vital role in strengthening national integration. By its deliberately planned programme, education can develop all aspects of a student's personality by broadening his out look, fostering a feeling of oneness and nationalism so that his narrow group interests surrendered in the larger interests of a country. This programme can be undertaken by adopting the following measures.

1. Re-Stating the Aims of Education
2. National System of Education
3. Method of Teaching
4. Role of Language
5. Co-curricular Activities
6. Educational Tours and Trips
7. Exchange Programmes
8. Teaching of Religion
9. Re-orienting Instruction in Social Science

History should reveal India's unity in diversity. Through geography the students may be made to realise the variety of peoples that inhabit it, their ways of like, their food habits etc.

Civics should be taught with a view of creating desirable attitudes for national unity and Emotional Integration. The study of art, literature and music also help to develop national consciousness.

10. Re-Designing the Curriculum

One of the aims of secondary education it self is national integration. The destiny of India is being shaped in her classrooms. Every subject must be taught from the point of view of national needs and achievements. There is a need to re-interpret the contents of various subjects in the light of larger interest of the nation.

National integration is vital for India's survival. It is the cry of the moment. In the words of our former Prime Minister Mrs. Indira Gandhi, "The question of national integration is serious enough to be studied calmly. It needs a deep conviction that this is the most urgent question of the day and also burning passion to summon all strength and will to surmount it by fighting all that leads to injustice, inequality and discrimination. Let us not degrade the very name of Indian citizenship.

11. Role of Teacher

Children are the most sensitive section of our community. They look to us for guidance and imitate our ways of life. Millions of children's eyes are focused on us and there are no eyes more observant, keen and perceptive than the eyes of a child. So if we really wish our children to be good, honest, brave, national minded and patriotic, we should have to get our example before then. Let you act up to brotherhood among your pupil.

REFERENCE

1. Thamarasssrei, Ismail (2008), *Education in the Emerging Indian Society*, New Delhi: Kanishka Publishers.

Eleventh Five-year Plan and Education

Elementary Education and Literacy

The role of education in facilitating social and economic progress is well recognised. It opens up opportunities leading to both individual and group entitlements. Education, in its broadest sense of development of youth, is the most crucial input for empowering people with skills and knowledge and giving them access to productive employment in future. Improvements in education are not only expected to enhance efficiency but also augment the overall quality of life. The Eleventh Plan places the highest priority on education as a central instrument for achieving rapid and inclusive growth. It presents a comprehensive strategy for strengthening the education sector covering all segments of the education pyramid.

Elementary education, that is, classes I-VIII consisting of primary (I-V) and upper primary (VI-VIII) is the foundation of the pyramid in the education system and has received a major push in the Tenth Plan through the Sarva Shiksha Abhiyan (SSA). In view of the demands of rapidly changing technology and the growth of knowledge economy, a mere eight years of elementary education would be grossly inadequate for our young children to acquire necessary skills to compete in the job market. Therefore, a Mission for Secondary Education is essential to consolidate the gains of SSA and to move forward in establishing a knowledge society. The Eleventh Plan must also pay attention to the problems in the higher education sector, where there is a need to expand the system and also to improve quality. The Eleventh Plan will also have to address major challenges including bridging regional, social, and gender gaps at all levels of education.

Elementary Education in the Tenth Plan

Major Schemes in the Tenth Plan

The Tenth Plan laid emphasis on Universalisation of Elementary Education (UEE) guided by five parameters:

1. Universal Access.
2. Universal Enrolment.
3. Universal Retention.
4. Universal Achievement.
5. Equity.

The major schemes of elementary education sector during the Tenth Plan included SSA, District Primary Education Programme (DPEP), National Programme of Nutritional Support to Primary Education, commonly known as Mid-Day Meal Scheme (MDMS), Teacher Education Scheme, and Kasturba Gandhi Balika Vidyalaya Scheme (KGBVS). The schemes of Lok Jumbish and Shiksha Karmi were completed but DPEP will extend up to November 2008. KGBV has now been subsumed within SSA.

Sarva Shiksha Abhiyan (SSA)

SSA, the principal programme for UEE, is the culmination of all previous endeavours and experiences in implementing various education programmes. While each of these programmes and projects had a specific focus – Operation Blackboard on improving physical infrastructure; DPEP on primary education; Shiksha Karmi Project on teacher absenteeism, and Lok Jumbish Project on girls' education – SSA has been the single largest holistic programme addressing all aspects of elementary education covering over one million elementary schools and Education Guarantee Centre (EGS)/ Alternate and Innovative Education (AIE) Centres and about 20 crore children.

Performance of SSA and Related Schemes in Tenth Plan

The specific goals of SSA during the Tenth Plan period were as follows:

- All children to be in regular school, EGS, AIE, or 'Back-to-School' camp by 2005.
- Bridging all gender and social category gaps at primary stage by 2007 and at elementary education level by 2010.
- Universal retention by 2010.
- Focus on elementary education of satisfactory quality with emphasis on education for life.

Universal Access

SSA has brought primary education to the doorstep of millions of children and enrolled them, including first generation learners, through successive fast track initiatives in hitherto unserved and under served habitations. According to the VII Educational Survey (2002), the number of habitations that had a primary school within a distance of 1 km was 10.71 lakh (87%), the uncovered habitations numbered 1.61 lakh (13%), whereas, the number of habitations that had an upper primary school within a distance of 3 km was 9.61 lakh (78%). With the opening up of 1.32 lakh primary schools and 56000 EGS/AIE centres access to primary education is nearly achieved. About 0.89 lakh upper primary schools (UPS) have been provided up to 2006-07. At primary and at upper primary level the number of habitations remaining to be covered is estimated at almost 1 lakh.

The number of primary schools (PS) in the country increased from 6.64 lakh in 2001-02 to 7.68 lakh in 2004-05. In the same period, the number of UPS increased at a faster rate from 2.20 lakh to 2.75 lakh. The sanction of 2.23 lakh new PS/UPS, 1.88 lakh new school buildings, and 6.70 lakh additional class rooms has made a big dent in reducing the school infrastructure gap.

Universal Enrolment

SSA had a sluggish start as States took considerable time to prepare district perspective plans. By the time the States realised the full potential of SSA, two and a half years had already rolled on. The urgency called for fast track initiatives. Household surveys, school mapping, constitution of Village Education Committees (VECs), setting up of Mother Teacher Associations and Parent Teacher Associations, and a series of campaigns for enrolment and context-specific strategies, all learnt from the experience of implementing DPEP, were used for good results in the next two and a half years. As a result, the second phase of enrolment drive by the States/union territories (UTs) was more systematic with household survey data reflecting substantially improved Gross Enrolment Ratio (GER) and a significant reduction in the number of out-of-school children. The strategy of providing AIE grants to Maktabs/Madarsas for introducing teaching of general subjects to minority children was also very fruitful.

Consequently, the total enrolment at elementary education level increased from 159 million in 2001-02 to 182 million in 2004-05, an increase of over 23 million.

Social and gender disparity, existing at both primary and upper primary education levels, continues to be an issue to be tackled with more concerted and sustained efforts, especially in Bihar, Rajasthan, Jharkhand, Madhya Pradesh (MP), Gujarat, and Uttar Pradesh (UP).

SSA interventions have brought down the number of out-of-school children from 32 million in 2001-02 to 7.0 million in 2006-07. 48 districts in 10 States accounted for over 50000 out-of-school children, each. The number of such districts declined to 29 in 2005-06. An independent study estimated that about 6.9 per cent of the total children in the 6-13 age groups were out of school and of them 2.1 per cent accounted for dropouts and 4.8 per cent for never-enrolled children, a bulk of whom apparently belonged to the poorer segments of rural households.

The social composition of out-of-school children indicates that 9.97 per cent of Muslim children, 9.54 per cent of Scheduled Tribes (STs), 8.17 per cent of Scheduled Castes (SCs), and 6.97 per cent of Other Backward Class (OBC) children were out of school and an overwhelming majority (68.7%) was concentrated in five States, *viz.*, Bihar (23.6%), UP (22.2%), West Bengal (WB) (9%), MP (8%), and Rajasthan (5.9%).

Universal Retention

It is increasingly realised that retaining the disadvantaged children enrolled in schools is a far more challenging task than enrolling them into educational system. Around 22 per cent children dropped out in classes I and II. Several factors, apart from their adverse socio-economic conditions are responsible for this. The opportunity cost of girl-child education is quite high in the rural set up and she is often a 'no where child', neither in the school nor in the labour force but doing domestic work, mostly sibling care. It is well documented that the presence of female teachers often serves as a role model for girls and positively influences their enrolment and attendance. But, then, in the educationally backward States, there are few women teachers to particularly attract girls to school and retain them.

SSA stipulates that 50 per cent of additionally recruited teachers should be women. Given the emphasis on improving girls' enrolment, which is critically dependent upon the presence of female teachers, there is a need to increase the proportion to 75 per cent in the recruitment of female teachers in educationally fragile States.

The fact that children drop out of school early or fail to acquire basic literacy and numeracy skills partially reflected poor quality of education. The average school attendance was around 70 per cent of the enrolment in 2004-05. In States like UP and Bihar, the average attendance was as low as 57 per cent and 42 per cent, respectively. One-third of the teachers in MP, 25 per cent in Bihar, and 20 per cent in UP don't attend schools.

Besides, the repetition rates in such States are also very high, resulting in wastage of human and material resources. Teacher attendance, ability, and motivation appear to be the weakest links of elementary education programmes. Lack of universal pre-schooling (Early Childhood Care and Education, ECCE) and consequent poor vocabulary and poor conceptual development of mind makes even enrolled children less participative in the class, even for learning by rote However, the dropout rate at the elementary level (classes I-VIII) has remained very high at 50.8 per cent.

The dropout rates at primary levels for SCs (34.2%) and STs (42.3%) are substantially higher than the national average (29%). The gap in respect of SCs is very wide in Goa, UP, Tamil Nadu, West Bengal, Haryana, and Himachal Pradesh. The gap in respect of STs is very large in Maharashtra, Andhra Pradesh, Orissa, and Gujarat. The social gap in dropout rate is acute in respect of girls. Two-thirds of the tribal students just do not go beyond class VIII.

Universal Achievement and Equity

Two major issues yet to be addressed satisfactorily under UEE are quality and equity. The results of learning achievement surveys conducted by National Council for Education Research and Training (NCERT) and also by independent agencies (Annual Status of Education Report, 2005) highlight poor quality of learning.

Eleventh Plan: Goals, Targets, and Strategies in Elementary Education

The Constitution of India was amended in 2002 to make elementary education a justiciable Fundamental Right. However, 7.1 million children being out of school and over 50 per cent dropping out at elementary level are matters of serious concern. SSA would, therefore, for Quality Elementary Education to ensure minimum norms and standards for schools (both governmentand private). It would address access, quality, and equity holistically though a systems approach. The backlog for additional classrooms is about 6.87 lakh. Opening of about 20000 new primary schools and up-gradation of about 70000 primary schools are required. Unless there is a strong effort to address the systemic issues of regular functioning of schools, teacher attendance and competence, accountability of educational administrators, pragmatic teacher transfer and promotion policies, effective decentralisation of school management, and transfer of powers to Panchayati Raj Institutions (PRIs), it would be difficult to build upon the gains of SSA. It is important to focus on good quality education of common standards, pedagogy, and syllabi to ensure minimum learning levels.

In the liberalised global economy where there is a pursuit for achieving excellence, the legitimate role of private providers of quality education not only needs to be recognised, but also encouraged. Public-Private Partnership (PPP) need not necessarily mean only seeking private investments to supplement governmental efforts, but also encouraging innovation in education that the government schools may lack. Schools under private management (unaided) have been expanding at a faster rate. However, a vast majority of the poor, particularly in rural areas, is solely dependent on government schools.

The substantial step up in the Eleventh Planoutlay in the Central sector would increasingly be invested in improving quality of elementary education, recruiting additional teachers (particularly science and mathematics), seeking technology up-gradation including ICT in schools, and Technical Assistance (TA) including the educationally fragile States. The issue of poor performing schools would be addressed by grading schools through a composite index and by providing TA.

It has been found that students who often don't perform well in conventional subject examinations demonstrate high success levels in the use of Information Technology (IT) and IT-enabled learning. IT could provide new directions in pedagogical practices and students' achievement. The idea is not merely making children computer literate but also initiating web-based learning through modern software facilities.

For Elementary Education

- Universal enrolment of 6-14 age group children including the hard to reach segment.
- Substantial improvement in quality and standards with the ultimate objective to achieve standards of Kendriya Vidyalayas (KVs) under the Central Board of Secondary Education (CBSE) pattern.
- All gender, social, and regional gaps in enrolments to be eliminated by 2011-12.
- One year pre-school education (PSE) for children entering primary school.
- Drop-out at primary level to be eliminated and the dropout rate at the elementary level to be reduced from over 50 per cent to 20 per cent by 2011-12.
- Universalised MDMS at elementary level by 2008-09.
- Universal coverage of ICT at UPS by 2011-12.
- Significant improvement in learning conditions with emphasis on learning basic skills, verbal and quantitative.
- All EGS centres to be converted into regular primary schools.
- All States/UTs to adopt NCERT Quality Monitoring Tools.
- Strengthened BRCs/CRCs: 1 CRC for every 10 schools and 5 resource teachers per block.

Quality Improvement in SSA

In the Eleventh Plan, the quality of education imparted in the primary and UPS would be improved through a range of coherent, integrated, and comprehensive strategies with clearly defined goals that help in measuring progress. These include the following:

- Restructure SSA with a clear goal of providing a quality of education equivalent to that of KVs under the CBSE pattern.
- Ensure basic learning conditions in all schools and acquisition of basic skills of literacy and numeracy in early primary grades to lay a strong foundation for higher classes.

- Universally introduce English in Class III onwards.
- Implement a Common Syllabi, Curriculum, and Pedagogy and carry out the consequent text-book revisions.
- Support more quality-related activities and improve interactive classroom transaction.
- Address fully all teacher-related issues – vacancies, absenteeism, non-teaching assignments, and fix accountability for learning outcomes of pupils.
- Achieve 100 per cent training for teachers including Para-teachers.
- Revise Pupil Teacher Ratio to 30:1 from 40:1.
- Recruit additional teachers to deal with single teacher schools and multi-grade teaching with mandatory two-third new teachers to be female for primary classes.
- National Eligibility Test (NET)/State Eligibility Test (SET) for teacher recruitment by NCERT/State Council for Educational Research and Training (SCERT)/CBSE/State Boards to enable decentralised recruitment of high-quality teaching faculty at district/block levels.
- Make District Institutes of Education and Training (DIETs)/SCERTs fully functional and organically linked with BRC/CRC and NCERT.
- Enhance learning levels by at least 50 per cent over baseline estimates (2005-06 District Information System for Education [DISE]).
- 'Improved Quality' to be defined in operational terms through clearly identified outcome indicators, *viz.*, learning levels of students, teacher competence, classroom processes, teaching learning materials, etc.
- The National Curriculum Framework (NCF) 2005 and the syllabi prepared by NCERT to be the guiding documents for States for revising their curricula/syllabi with SCERTs playing a more active role in ensuring common standard.
- Introduce monetary and non-monetary incentives for recognising good teachers with block/district and State awards.

- Sharing of SSA Expenditure and Reprioritisation of SSA Components.

The approved SSA programme provided for an 85:15 sharing between Centre and the States till the end of the Ninth Plan period, 75:25 sharing during the Tenth Plan period, and 50:50 there after. In view of persistent demand from the States and the urgency in filling up the infrastructure gap in the educationally fragile States, the funding pattern between Centre and States/UTs for SSA Phase II has been modified to 65:35 for the first two years of the Eleventh Plan, 60:40 for the third year, 55:45 for the fourth year, and 50:50 thereafter. The special dispensation for NE States during 2005-06 and 2006-07 will continue for the Eleventh Plan whereby each of the NE States contributes only 10 per cent of the approved outlay as State share.

The restructuring of SSA will include ensuring that all teachers, including para teachers, are trained, the norms for civil works are the same throughout a State, there is 1 CRC for every 10 schools, 10 CRCs per BRC, and 5 resource teachers per block, there is no single teacher school and no multi-grade teaching. The curricula/syllabi will be revised as per the NCF and the NCERT guidelines.

Special Interventions for the Disadvantaged Groups

Young learners from socially marginalised sections experience education in a distinctly different form than those who occupy mainstream positions of power and privilege. They face overt and covert forms of rejection in schooling. The Eleventh Plan will lay special focus on disadvantaged groups and educationally backward areas. This focus will include not only higher resource allocation but also capacity building for preparation and implementation of strategies based on identified needs, more intensive monitoring and supervision, and tracking of progress. Specific measures will include:

- Top priority in pre-primary schooling to habitations of marginalised sections.

- Higher concentration of SC, ST, OBC, and minority population.
- Special attention to districts with high SCs, STs, and minority population. Innovative funds for SFDs to be doubled.
- Focus on improving the learning levels of SC, ST, minority children through remedial coaching in schools and also in habitations through educated youth of Nehru Yuva Kendra Sangathan (NYKS), NSS, Self-help Groups (SHGs), and local non-governmental organizations (NGOs).
- Special schools for slum children in 35 cities with million plus population.
- Special intervention for migrating children, deprived children in urban slum areas, single parent's children, physically challenged children, and working children.
- Creation of capacity within the school for dealing with students lagging in studies.
- Setting up 1000 hostels in EBBs with the resident PG teacher as the warden to provide supplementary academic support.
- Sensitising teachers for special care of weaker sections and CWSN.
- Intensive social mobilisation in SCs, STs, OBCs, and predominantly tribal and minority habitations through community support.
- Housing for teachers in tribal and remote habitations.

Pre-school Education (PSE)

The PSE component of ICDS-Anganwadi is very weak with repetition high and learning levels low. This in turn discourages many children from continuing their education. SSA will have a component of one year pre-primary, which can be universalised to cover 2.4 crore children in a phased manner. This is critical for school readiness/entry with increased basic vocabulary and conceptual abilities that help school retention. Besides, it will free the girl child of sibling care. The existing coverage of pre-primary classes in schools is over 11 million. A large number of primary schools in States like UP and Rajasthan already have ECCE. Primary schools within the habitations are ideal for such ECCE. In other habitations, ICDS-Anganwadi will be supported.

Madarsas/Maktabs

In the Eleventh Plan additional madarsa maktabs will be supported for modernisation under AIE component and it should be possible to cover all the 12000 odd Madarsas during the Plan period.

Education in human moral values, civic duties, environmental protection, and physical education will be built into the system whereby every child is prepared to face the future with a healthy frame of mind and body and become a responsible citizen. Education will foster the spirit of liberty, freedom, patriotism, non-violence, tolerance, national unity and integration, cultural harmony, inquisitive reasoning, rationality, and scientific temper in young minds. Every school and EGS/AIE centre will receive a special grant to celebrate national festivals of Independence Day and Republic Day. Hoisting of national flag on these days should be made mandatory in all educational institutions including private schools with discipline.

KGBV and DPEP

These schemes will be subsumed within SSA in the Eleventh Plan. Expansion of 500 KGB Vs in district/blocks with high concentration of SCs, STs, OBCs, and minorities will be taken up. Also, an in-depth evaluation of the functioning of the existing KGB Vs will be under taken. The programme of civil works under KGBV appears to be slow in many States. DPEP will end in November 2008 and will be subsumed under SSA as per the existing procedure. The external commitments will however be met.

Mid-Day Meal Scheme (MDMS)

The scheme has been extended to UPS (government, local body, and government-aided schools, and EGS/AIE centres) in 3479 EBBs from 1 October 2002 to cover 17 million additional children and will be extended to all UPS from April 2008 to cover 54 million children. Thus, MDMS will cover about 18 crore children by 2008-09. The nutritional value of meals for upper primary children will be fixed at protein.

MDMS: Action Points

- MDM to be managed by the local community and PRIs/ NGOs, and not contractor-driven: civic quality and safety to be prime considerations.
- Sensitise teachers and others involved in nutrition, hygiene, cleanliness, and safety norms to rectify observed deficiencies.
- Involve nutrition experts in planning low cost nutrition menu and for periodic testing of samples of prepared food.
- Promote locally grown nutritionally rich food items through kitchen gardens in school, etc.
- Revive the School Health Programme; disseminate and replicate best practices adopted by States.
- Provide drinking facilities in all schools on an urgent basis.
- Display status regarding supplies, funds, norms, weekly menu, and coverage in schools to ensure transparency.
- Central assistance to cooking cost should be based on the actual number of beneficiary children and not on enrolment.
- Promote social audit.
- Online monitoring.

Mahila Samakhya (MS)

The MS programme will be continued as per the existing pattern and expanded in a phased manner to cover all the EBBs and also in urban/suburban slums, as it contributes to educational empowerment of poor women. There is a need to operationalise the National Resource Centre of MS to support training, research, and proper documentation. The documentation and dissemination of MS needs its strengthening. It is desirable to conclude negotiations with the development partners as EAP comes with excellent project design and measurement system, capacity building, and TA.

Literacy and Adult Education: Performance in Tenth Plan

Literacy is the most essential prerequisite for individual empowerment. A new thrust was given to adult literacy in the National Policy on Education 1986 and the Plan of Action 1992, which advocated a three-pronged strategy of adult education, elementary education, and non-formal education to eradicate illiteracy. The National Literacy Mission (NLM) was set up in 1988 with an initial target to make 80 million persons literate by 1995, which was later enhanced to 100 million by 1997 and the revised target is to achieve a threshold level of 75 per cent literacy by 2007.

Dominant strategies of the NLM and the Total Literacy Campaigns (TLC) were 'area specific, time bound, volunteer based, cost effective and result oriented. 'The efforts made by the TLCs and Post Literacy Projects (PLP) to eradicate illiteracy yielded commendable results: rise in literacy from 52.2 per cent in 1991 to 64.8 per cent in 2001. The urban-rural literacy differential also decreased during the period. The literacy rates for females increased at a faster rate than that for males. However, gender and regional disparities in literacy still continue to persist. The national overall literacy rate for Muslims is 59.1 per cent (males 67.6% and females 50.1%). The literacy rate among Muslims is higher than the national literacy rate of 64.8 per cent in 17 States/UTs. Female literacy rates among Muslims are particularly low in Haryana (21.5%), Bihar (31.5%), Nagaland (33.3%), and Jammu and Kashmir (34.9%).

The Tenth Plan had set a target of achieving a sustainable threshold level of 75 per cent literacy by 2007, to cover all left-over districts by 2003-04, to remove residual illiteracy in the existing districts by 2004-05, to complete PLP in all districts and to launch Continuing Education Programmes (CEP) in 100 districts by the end of the Plan period TLC and PLP.

The TLC has been the principal strategy of NLM for eradication of illiteracy. The TLCs are implemented through Zilla Saksharata Samitis (District Literacy Societies), independent and autonomous bodies having due representation of all sections of society. A total of 597 districts are presently covered under various literacy programmes. The Central:State share for TLCs and PLPs is in the ratio of 2:1 for general districts and Education for tribal districts. During the Tenth Plan period, the total number of districts under TLC and PLP were 95 and 174, respectively.

As per 2001 census, 47 districts had a female literacy rate below 30 per cent. These districts are concentrated in UP, Bihar, Orissa, and Jharkhand. Special Innovative programmes were taken up in identified districts for improvement of female literacy. In many cases despite the completion of the TLC campaigns, a large number of illiterates remained unreached. Projects for Residual Illiteracy were launched after the conclusion of TLCs for covering the remaining illiterates in districts of Rajasthan (10), Andhra Pradesh (8), Bihar (4), Jharkhand (3), MP (9), Karnataka (2), UP (13), and West Bengal (4).

Special Literacy Drive in 150 Districts

A special literacy drive was launched in 150 districts in April 2005, which had the lowest literacy rates in the country. These districts are mainly in UP, Bihar, Jharkhand, Rajasthan, MP, Chhattisgarh, and Orissa. The special drive aimed to cover nearly 36 million illiterates during 2005-07. So far, 134 districts have been completed.

Continuing Education Programme (CEP)

The Continuing Education Scheme provides a learning continuum to the efforts made by TLC/PLP. The main thrust is on providing further learning opportunities to neo-literates by setting up Continuing Education Centres that provide area-specific and need-based opportunities for basic literacy, up-gradation of literacy skills, pursuit of alternative educational programmes, vocational skills, and promotion of social and occupational development. The total number of districts covered under CEP is 328.

Jan Shikshan Sansthan (JSS)

The objective of JSS Scheme is educational, vocational, and occupational development of socio-economically backward and educationally disadvantaged groups of urban/rural population, particularly neo-literates, semi-literates, SCs, STs, women and girls, slum dwellers, migrant workers, etc. By linking literacy with vocational training, JSSs seek to improve the quality of life of the beneficiaries. JSSs offered around 284 different types of vocational courses – from candle and agarbatti making to computer training and hospital/health care. The total number of JSSs is 198.

Major Weaknesses in Adult Education Programmes

The constraints in the implementation of adult education programmes include inadequate participation of the State Governments, low motivation and training of voluntary teachers, lack of convergence of programmes under CEP, and weak management and supervision structure for implementation for NLM. Besides, the funding for various components of NLM schemes was also inadequate and the level of community participation was low.

REFERENCE

1. http://planningcommission.nic.in/sectors/index.php?sectors=edu®

20

Education, Equality and Social Justice

An Indian Scenario

India is a diverse country with one of the oldest civilizations of the world. With its rich cultural heritage, it has traversed a long distance during the last sixty one years of its independence. Though it accounts for 2.4 per cent of the world surface area, it supports 16.7 per cent of the world population. India with its mammoth population, 1.28 billion, lives in 28 States and 7 Union Territories. The uniqueness of the Indian society is 'Unity in Diversity', which is visible in its religions, languages, cultures and castes. India is a multireligious country with Hindus accounting for 80.5 per cent, Muslims 13.43 per cent, Christian 2.3 per cent and others, constituting an important part of Indian diversity, accounting for the rest. Hindi in the 'devanagari' script is the official language of the country but both Hindi and English are collectively used by the Union Government for certain specified administrative purposes. Besides, the eighth schedule of the Indian Constitution recognises as many as 22 scheduled languages. By some count, there are over 200 languages and almost 1,600 dialects that are spoken in the country.

The Education system of a country does not function in isolation from the society of which it is a part. Hierarchies of castes, economic status, gender relations and cultural diversities as well as uneven economic development also deeply influence issues relating to access and equity in education. Our society has been characterised with deeply entrenched social inequalities between various social groups and castes since ancient times. Though India was widely acclaimed as a land of knowledge and wisdom during ancient times yet access to education was limited to select strata of the society. The marginalised groups of the society were subjected to social and economic oppression. These centuries old social prejudices and inequalities, based on caste at birth, continue to dog the modern Indian landscape. Extending educational opportunities to the marginalised groups was considered an antidote to this long-standing discrimination. Several attempts have been made by social reformers and others to make education accessible to these marginal groups with varying degree of success.

This unit discusses the constitutional provisions for education, equality and social justice as also critically examines the current educational status including that of SCs, STs, OBCs, minority groups and women at all levels of education. The policy interventions with the special reference to above stated social groups have been insightfully examined in the paper. It also discusses the significance and impact of affirmative policy interventions, key concerns which continue to confront the country in assuring access and equity in education. It gives broad directions on the milestones which define the way forward to meet the emerging challenges of providing equality of opportunity and social justice through the instrumentality of educational interventions.

Constitutional Provisions for Education, Equality and Social Justice

The Indian Constitution enacted in 1949 and adopted in 1950 enshrines equality and social justice as the cardinal principles of the Indian democratic system. The unique feature of the Indian Constitution is that while it upholds the principle of equality before law, it provides for affirmative discriminatory actions to uplift the social, economic and educational well-being of disadvantaged groups. The Constitution recognises the Scheduled Castes (SCs), Scheduled Tribes (STs) and educationally Other Backward Classes (OBCs), Minorities and Women as disadvantaged groups. The ultimate objective of the Constitution Framers was to establish a casteless society within the framework of a welfare state by gradually eliminating caste hierarchy, caste distinction and caste stigma and thus to ensure the dignity of the individual and equality of status among all the citizens of India. The Preamble of the Constitution assures Justice, social, economic and political, as well as Equality of status and of opportunity with a view to promoting among all citizens Fraternity, assuring the dignity of the individual and the unity and integrity of the nation. These ideals are clearly reflected in different clauses of the Constitution. Article 14 guarantees equality before the law and the equal protection of law to all persons. Article 15(1) prohibits discrimination against any citizen on grounds of religion, race, caste or sex. Article 16(1) guarantees equality of opportunity for all citizens in matters relating to employment or appointment to any office under the State.

In order to make the Fundamental Rights referred to above meaningful to the socially disadvantaged people of this country, particularly those who had been badly maltreated and subjugated to social injustices for centuries, the Constitution makers made several provisions in the constitution to raise their level so that they may live with dignity and respect. Article 17 provides for abolition of untouchability, and the enforcement of any disability arising from it was made punishable as an offence according to law.

Article 15(4) was not there initially in the Constitution when it was enacted and was introduced as a first amendment to the Constitution. It enabled the government to make special provisions for the advancement of backward classes including the Scheduled Castes (SCs) and Scheduled Tribes (STs). As per Article 16(4), the Government can make reservations in favour of any backward class of citizens.

Political representation was guaranteed for SCs and STs through the proportionate reservation of seats in all elected legislative bodies from Parliament to Village Councils. Not only that, the Government of India instituted a programme of 'Compensatory discrimination', an Indian version of affirmative action, which provides for 15 per cent reservation to SCs and 7.5 per cent reservation to STs in all public services as well as in admissions to all public universities and colleges. Article 46 of the Constitution clearly states that the State shall promote with special care the educational and economic interests of the weaker sections of the people, and, in particular, of the SCs and the STs, and shall protect them from social injustice and all forms of exploitation. The 86th Amendment to the Constitution inserting Article 21A, in 2002, making elementary education a fundamental right is going to make positive impact on the education of SCs, STs, OBCs and women.

Besides, the National Policy on Education (1968) calls for strenuous efforts to correct regional imbalances and inter-group disparities in education. Reinforcing the 1968 Resolutions, the National Policy on Education and Programme of Action (1968/92) laid emphasis on the removal of disparities and equalisation of educational opportunities by attending to the specific needs of those who have been denied equality so far. Both the Policies have dealt with the educational needs of the SCs, STs, Women and Minorities in great detail with a special concern for neglected groups like nomadic tribes and de-notified tribes. Based on the constitutional commitment and policy directives, planned efforts have been made since independence to promote educational development in equitable manner. Consequently, there has been considerable improvement in the educational status of the deprived groups.

Protective Measures for Inclusivity

Other Backward Classes (OBCs)

The Government of India set up the Kaka Kelkar Commission in 1952 with a view to identifying the OBCs and giving them similar benefits as it had extended to SCs and STs. The Commission submitted its report in 1955 but its recommendations were contested in the courts until the Supreme Court ruled in 1963 that total reservation, inclusive of the quantum for SCs and STs could not exceed 50 per cent. Nothing happened for the next 15 years. It was in 1978 that the Government of India decided to set up the Second Backward Classes Commission under the Chairmanship of Mr. B.P. Mandal. The Commission aimed at providing affirmative action policies for backward and disadvantaged castes in order to redress caste discrimination. The Commission used as many as 11 indicators to determine the backwardness. The Commission identified 3,743 castes and communities, constituting 52 per cent of the total population, as OBCs. Driven by the 1963 Judgement of the Supreme Court, the Commission recommended 27 per cent reservation to OBCs in all services and public sector undertakings under the Central Government. It also recommended 27 per cent reservation to OBCs in admission to all public institutions of higher learning. Though the report of the Commission was submitted in 1978, it took 12 years for the government to implement its recommendations. In August 1990, The Government of India announced the implementation of the Commission's recommendation. The announcement met with tremendous resistance, and a writ petition was filed in the Supreme Court against the implementation of the Commission's recommendations. The Supreme Court, however, in its judgment (November 16, 1992) upheld 27 per cent reservations in services for OBCs. Subsequently, the Central Government introduced the Bill. The Central Educational Institutions (Reservation in Admission) Bill No. 76 of 2006 in the Parliament made 93rd Constitutional Amendment which provided for the reservation in admission of the students belonging to SCs, STs and OBCs to educational institutions established, maintained or aided by the Central Government, and for matters connected therewith or incidental there to. The Bill was passed by both the Lower House and the Upper House of the Parliament on December 14 and 18, 2006 respectively. No sooner had the Bill received an assent of the President and became the Central Educational Institutions

(Reservation in Admissions) Act, 2007 than its Constitutional validity was challenged in the Supreme Court. The Supreme Court in its judgment delivered on April 10, 2008 upheld the 93rd Amendment to the Constitution enabling the Government to reserve 27 per cent OBC quota in all centrally funded institutions of higher learning.

Minority Muslim Community

The Muslim community in India constitutes 13.43 per cent of the total population. Article 29 provides the minorities the right to conserve their language, script and culture. Article 30 gives the right to the minorities to establish and administer educational institutions of their choice. It has been expressed that amongst the minorities which have suffered educationally, the sense of inequity may be perpetual as a result of discrimination that the minority may face due to difference in 'identity'. In this connection, the Government of India is initiating several measures to bring about qualitative improvement in the status of the Muslim community. The present government in the centre has created a new 'Ministry of Minority Affairs' which has been entrusted with the responsibility of overall policy, planning, co-ordination, evaluation and review of the regulatory and developmental programmes of the minority communities. The same government through an Act of Parliament has also established the National Commission for Minority Educational Institutions on 11th November, 2004 to advise the central or any state government on any question relating to education of minorities. It has to look specific complaints regarding deprivation or violation of rights of minorities to establish and administer educational institutions of their choice and dispute relating affiliation to a scheduled university and has to do other acts and things necessary, incidental or conducive to the attainment of all or any of the objects of the commission.

The government has also set up a 'National Monitoring Committee for Minorities Education (NMCME)' under the chairmanship of Union Minister for Human Resource Development (MHRD) in the year 2004. A Standing Committee of the NMCME has also been constituted to attend to the problems related to the education of minorities on an ongoing basis. Not only that the Government of India also set up a higher powered Committee to understand social, economic and educational status of the Muslim community in India under the Chairpersonship of Justice Rajindar Sachar in 2005. The report consolidates, collates and analyses information with regard to the states, the regions, the districts and blocks where Muslims of India mostly live; geographical pattern of their economic activities; income levels; level of their socio-economic development; relative share in public and private sector employment; proportion of OBCs from the Muslim community in total OBC population. Information on these aspects has been indicated in the report of this committee to identify areas of interventions by the government to address relevant issues relating to the social, economic and educational status of the Muslim community. Besides, the Prime Minister has also introduced a new 15 point programme, for the welfare of minorities, which relate to enhancing opportunities for their education, equitable share in economic activities and employment, improving the conditions of living of minorities and prevention and control of communal riots.

Articles 350(A) advocates instruction in mother tongue at primary stage and Article 350(B) provides for a special officer to safeguard the interests of linguistic minorities. Further, the Constitution of India in its 'Union', 'State' and 'Concurrent List' defines the powers and functions of the Centre and the States. Under the Constitution originally adopted, education was primarily a State subject. Since this led to differential educational progress across the States, education was transferred to the Concurrent List through a Constitutional Amendment in 1976, which implies meaningful partnership between the Centre and the States. Though this shift did not change the role and responsibility of the States, it gave the Central Government a major role in strengthening the education system in the country. Since then, a large number of schemes and programmes in the form of affirmative policy interventions have been launched by the Central Government in collaboration with the State Governments to overcome the inadequacies hindering the educational progress. Consequently, the age-old discriminatory practices have nearly vanished. The educational status of marginal groups has greatly improved compared to the situation before country's independence.

Current Educational Scenario

Population and Literacy

India is a country with more than one billion people. Its population has experienced higher growth rates since independence largely owing to declining child and adult mortality rates as a result of improvement in health facilities and awareness. The growth and composition of population in India. It may be noted that the composition of population is mildly changing in favour of SCs and STs. The proportion of SCs increased from 14.7 per cent in 1961 to 16.2 per cent in 2001. Similarly the proportion of ST also slightly increased from 6.8 to 8.2 per cent between 1961 and 2001. The literacy rate of population including those of marginal groups has improved a lot. For example, in case of SCs, the literacy rate has increased from a little over 10 per cent in 1961 to 55 per cent in 2001. In case of STs, it increased from less than 9 per cent to 47 per cent during the same period. The process of collection of data on socio-economic and educational status of minority muslim community has commenced from 2001 Census. According to the latest figures, muslim literacy stands at 59.13 per cent. The literacy rate with respect to total population has increased from 28.3 per cent to 65.4 per cent between 1961 and 2001. Though these are laudable achievements, the country has to make concerted efforts to make all people literate.

Educational Attainment of Population aged 15 years and above

As mentioned earlier, extending educational facilities to marginal groups forms the core of approach of the Government of India to operationalise the Constitutional provisions of equality of opportunity and social justice. The state has been striving to provide elementary schools in each and every habitation with special attention to the SC and ST dominant habitations. The number of secondary and higher education institutions has also been on an increase to provide easy access. Further, scholarships, fee waivers, incentives, and finally reservation provisions have been instituted to achieve social justice and equality of opportunity. One moot question is what impact these measures have on the educational credentials possessed by different social groups. Is the distribution of education credentials equitable?

An examination of educational attainments of adults, more than 15 year of age, of various social groups throws up some interesting trends. Depicts proportion of people above 15 years of age who possess a particular level of education by social groups, gender and rural and urban. It unambiguously establishes wide inequalities between social groups. It also hints a hierarchy sort of thing between social groups in the possession of educational credentials. At the bottom end are ST rural females with more than 70 per cent illiterate. The proportion of ST rural females with secondary and higher qualification is absolutely miniscule with 4.4 per cent mark. At the other end of spectrum are urban other males with a little over 60 per cent having secondary and above qualifications. The illiterates constitute a miniscule 7.5 per cent among urban other males. Indicates that the educational status of SCs and STs particularly females living in rural areas has not changed much as significant proportions of them are either illiterate or have bare minimum educational attainments.

It is also documents some positive impact of policy interventions and other developments on educational attainment of marginal groups. For example, higher percentage of urban ST and SC males, 40 and 30.4 per cent respectively, possess secondary and above qualifications compared to only 31 per cent among rural other males (*i.e.,* non SC and ST). However, urban SC and ST males are a way behind the urban other males. This makes it amply clear that despite large expansion of educational facilities, the educational attainments of marginal groups continue to be very low.

Growth of Educational Institutions

The educational system has greatly expanded since independence to cater to the needs of all sections of society. Educational expansion was aimed at meeting the needs of growing economy and to foster equality among different sections of population. Accordingly, the educational needs of marginal groups like SCs and STs were addressed by opening educational institutions at elementary and secondary level in habitations dominated by them. The primary schools have grown by nearly four folds from 210 thousand in 1950-51 to 772 thousand schools in 2005-06. Similarly the number of upper primary and high/higher secondary schools has gone up by more than 20 times during the same period. The upper primary schools have gone up from 13 thousand schools to 288 thousand. The high/higher secondary schools have gone up from 7.4 thousand to 160 thousands during the same period.

The higher education sector has also witnessed a steep increase during this period. The colleges have gone by more than 30 times from merely 578 colleges in 1950-51 to nearly 21 thousand colleges in 2005-06. Universities and other institutions of higher learning have also gone up from 28 in 1950-51 to 416 in 2005-06. The education sector is further poised to grow during the XI Five-year Plan (FYP) which aims at inclusive growth. The expansion of educational opportunities at all levels of education with an emphasis on marginal groups is the key to strategies adopted to promote inclusive growth.

Participation in School Education

Enrolment at Primary and Upper Primary Stages

The efforts made by the Government of India to improve the participation levels of children of SCs and STs is reflected in the increased enrolment and higher growth rates of enrolment at primary and upper primary levels of education. The SC enrolment at primary level has increased by 2.3 times from 11 million in 1980-81 to 25.2 million in 2005-06. During the same period, ST enrolment at primary level has increased by three times. It has increased from 4.7 million in 1980-81 to

14.2 million in 2005-06. It is heartening to note that at primary level the enrolment of SCs and STs has grown at much higher pace by 2.3 and 3.0 times respectively compared to 1.8 times with respect to enrolment of general population between 1980-81 and 2005-06. The data also reveals that SC and ST enrolment at primary level has increased at an annual rate of growth of 3.38 per cent and 4.55 per cent respectively. It is also encouraging to note that growth rate in case of girl's enrolment at primary level is much higher than the total enrolment with respect to SCs and STs. Further, it is observed that SC and ST enrolment has registered higher growth rate at upper primary level than at the primary. The SC enrolment at upper primary level has increased at an annual growth rate of 5.82 per cent while that of ST at 7.46 per cent. In absolute terms, SC enrolment at upper primary level has increased from 2.22 million in 1980-81 to 9.14 million in 2005-06; thus showing an increase of more than 4 times. The ST enrolment at upper primary level has increased from 0.74 million in 1980-81 to 4.48 million in 2005-06 thus registering a little more than 6 times growth.

- *Elementary Education:* Similarly, the enrolment at elementary level also increased manifold. For example, the enrolment of SCs and STs increased by 3.5 and 2.6 times respectively compared to 2.0 times for general population between 1980-81 and 2005-06. The proportion of SCs in the total enrolment increased from 14 per cent in 1980-81 to 19 per cent and that of STs from 5.71 to 10.11 during the same period. The higher growth rates of enrolment of SCs and STs may help reduce the social gaps.
- *Secondary Education:* The secondary education is emerging as one of the critical areas of action in the changing global political economy. The access to and inequalities at secondary education are found to determine the subsequent life chances (Jaffery, 2005). Unfortunately, the spread of secondary education is very thin. It is, therefore, necessary to examine who is getting secondary education and who is not. It is worth mentioning that

the enrolment of marginal groups in secondary education is growing at a faster rate than the general population. For example, the enrolment of SC and ST girls is growing by more than 9 per cent per annum compared to a little over 6 per cent in case of girls of general population. Similarly, the enrolment of SCs and STs is growing at a higher rate of over 6 per cent per annum compared to a little higher than 5 per cent in case of general population. In absolute terms, the growth of enrolment is stupendous. It tripled between 1980-81 and 2005-06 from 11 million to 38.45 million. In a similar vein the enrolment of SCs and STs also increased by 4.5 and 6.3 times from 1.2 and 0.3 million to 5.6 and 2.2 million respectively during the same period.

Gross Enrolment Ratio at School Level

The Gross Enrolment Ratio (GER) is one crude indicator that gives some idea about the coverage of corresponding age population at different levels of school education. Though the GER has been increasing since independence, it falls short of expectations and the needs of growing economy. The manifold increase in enrolment is reflected in the substantial improvement of GER which for SCs and STs is well over 100 per cent. Computational and data base problems make it difficult to derive any meaningful trends in what appears to be a rather haphazard movement in GER at primary level of education. However, one unmistakable trend, which one can discern, is the large scale participation of children of SCs and STs in primary education. The high GER values for both SCs (118%) and STs (126%) stand testimony to this. It is interesting to note that the current GER values in respect of SCs and STs even surpass the GER of general population (109%). Needless to mention that a higher GER for marginalised sections such as SC and ST population may not necessarily be interpreted as higher levels of participation of corresponding age children because of under-age and over-age children and often it is the children belonging to these marginalised sections who tend to be over-aged corresponding to the grade.

At the upper primary level also, the GER for SCs and STs has significantly improved over a period of time. The GER for SCs and STs have improved from 52.7 per cent and 40.7 per cent in 1990-91 to 73.4 per cent and 71.7 per cent in 2004-05 respectively. The disparities between general population and that for SCs and STs have virtually vanished. Despite this improvement, it may be noted that GER at upper primary level is still low not only for SCs and STs butal so for general population. It is important to recognize that the absence of disparities in GER between general population and SCs and STs does not necessarily mean equal participation. As noted earlier, the GER includes under and over aged children and these children are likely to disproportionately belong to SCs and STs. As a result, the disparities may show up in net participation levels but unfortunately, the data are not available. Thus increasing the participation of children in upper primary level of education and also ensuring equity by focusing on SCs and STs is emerging as one of the significant policy concerns in the achievement of universal elementary education. This clearly suggests that lot more needs to be done to achieve Universalisation of Elementary Education (UEE) as enshrined in the Constitution with full regards to the implications of Article 21A making education a Fundamental Right.

Though the GER at secondary level has increased from very low levels, it still continues to be very low across all groups of population. The GER has increased from 32 per cent in 1990-91 to about 41 per cent even in 2005-06. Besides, one can also notice large inequalities between various social groups in the participation in secondary education. The GER for SCs and STs at secondary level stands at 37 and 29 per cent in 2005-06. This clearly demonstrates that the expansion of secondary education has not only been very limited but also unequal. As only people with secondary and above qualifications can deal with the emerging global knowledge economy, it is imperative to expand school education and achieve universal elementary as well as secondary education simultaneously. It is ill advised to hold back the expansion of one level of education to expand another level of education. It is necessary that the universalisation of elementary and secondary education should not be seen as competitors but as complementary as it eventually supports each other.

- *Dropouts at School Level:* Pre-mature withdrawal of children from school is rampant in India. Without reversing this trend it is difficult to achieve universal elementary and secondary education. The Government has taken several steps like providing incentives, making school attractive by equipping it with teaching-learning material, reforming teaching methods, making transition from one school to another school easy, etc., to retain children in the system till they complete the specific cycle. Indeed, these initiatives have had positive impact though partially. The dropout rates have come down from 65 per cent in 1960-61 to 43 per cent in 1990-91 and further to 25.5 per cent in 2005-06 between classes I and V.

The dropout rate has registered large decline since 1990s that can be attributed to the efforts made under District Primary Education Programme (DPEP), SSA and other programmes. With respect to SC children, the dropout between classes I and V declined from 50 per cent in 1990-91 to 33.8 per cent in 2005-06. Similarly with respect to ST children it declined from 62.5 per cent to 39.8 per cent during the same period. Between 2001-02 and 2005-06, *i.e.,* within a span of five years, the dropout rate at primary level was brought down by more than 10 percentage points for both SC and ST children. The decline is very steep particularly from 2001 suggesting that the efforts made under SSA are making a dent. The proportion of children who dropout before reaching class VIII and X has also declined substantially. It declined from 61 per cent in 1990-91 to 49 per cent in 2005-06 with respect to class VIII for children of general population. With respect to class X, it declined from 71 to 62 per cent for the children of general population during the same period. Unfortunately the dropout rates of children of SCs and STs at classes VIII and X continued unabated. In 2005-06, the dropout rates are as high as 55 per cent for SCs and 63 per cent for STs at classes VIII and 71 per cent for SCs and 79 per cent for STs at Classes X. However, it shows a decline of 12 percentage points for SCs and 15 percentage point for STs at class VIII between 1990-91 and 2005-06 and a decline of 7 percentage points for SCs and 6 percentage point for STs at class X.

The above discussion unambiguously suggests that the action must now be taken at upper primary and secondary level to ensure that the gains made at primary education are consolidated and the existing gaps are further narrowed down. Perhaps an SSA sort of intensive programme with research-based interventions must be designed which could address the local contextualities.

Another point that is emerging strongly from the foregoing discussion is the contribution of large decreases in dropout rates of SC and ST children at primary education and narrowing down of disparities between these children and the children of general population in the recent past. Similar reduction has not taken place at upper primary and secondary level not only with respect to SCs and STs but also with respect to general population. As a result, the participation rates in secondary education continue to be low for all social groups. Further, the disparity between general population and SCs and STs remained high at upper primary and secondary level. Thus it suggests that the low participation levels of children in upper primary and secondary education and inequalities are not different problems but two sides of the same coin. It suggests that an appropriate policy ought to be designed in such a manner that it not only increases the participation rates of all groups of children but also reduces disparities amongst them at the same time.

- *Gender Parity at School Level:* Without removing gender disparities it is impossible to achieve universal elementary and secondary education. It is generally observed that girls are at a disadvantage due to several economic, cultural and social factors. A sizeable number of girl populationis engaged in carrying out domestic chores. Some of them are prevented from attending school due to social pressures. Some are forced to discontinue studies on attainment of puberty. The Government of India has launched several initiatives to improve the enrolment as also attendance rates of girls. Some of those measures are like scholarships and fee waivers, free education up to college and even higher, separate toilets for girls, appointment of female teachers. Indeed, the enrolment of girls has improved quite a lot during the last couple of years. The gender gap has completely vanished at primary level and significantly reduced at upper primary and secondary level. For example, the GER for girls increased from 25 per cent in 1950-51 to over 100 per cent in 2005-06 at primary level. Similarly it increased from 4.6 per cent in 1950-51 to 67 per cent in 2005-06 at upper primary level. At secondary level, it increased from 4.6 per cent in 1960-61 to 36 per cent in 2005-06. However, the gender gap at upper primary and secondary levels is declining tardily and continues to be very high. The gender gap with respect to SCs and STs is even higher. Gender equality is normally expressed with the help of gender parity index.

The trends in gender parity index are positive on account of several interventions mentioned earlier. The gender parity index has improved from 0.75 in 1990-91 to 0.94 in 2005-06 for general population at primary level. Similar improvements can be discerned for SCs and STs as well. For example, it increased from 0.69 to 0.87 for SCs and from 0.65 to .90 for STs at primary level during the same period. The gender parity index has moved up significantly at upper primary and secondary levels. It is 0.88 and 0.80 in 2005-06 compared to 0.61 and 0.59 in 1990-91 at upper primary and secondary levels respectively. The gender parity with respect to SCs and STs moved up from 0.52 to 0.80 and 0.50 to 0.84 respectively between 1990-91 and 2005-06 at upper primary level. At secondary level, non-availability of data precludes examining long-term trends in gender parity for SCs and STs but the latest figures suggest large gender gap. The gender parity index is found to be 0.74 and 0.69 for SCs and STs respectively in 2005-06.

Measure of Social Equality at School Level

The comparison of GER of various social groups reveals the inequalities between them. However, it is useful and easy to comprehend if we can express the inequality with single indicator. An attempt has been made here. The social equality index has been defined as the ratio of NER of marginal groups to general (average of) population. If participation level of marginal groups equals the average participation level of population, then social equality index takes the value of 1. If no one from marginal groups enters the education system (NER is zero) then social equality index takes the value of zero. The equality index for advanced groups exceeds one. As the data on NER are not available we have substituted it with GER. The social equality index is found to be higher than one at primary level. This implies that the disparities between different social groups have nearly vanished as mentioned earlier. Similar is the case at upper primary level. However, one can notice lower social parity measure at secondary education level. The social parity measure at secondary level is found to be 0.91 for SCs and 0.71 for STs in 2005-06. As the under and over age children tend to be higher in marginal groups, the social parity may likely to be much lower than these numbers suggest.

Policy Interventions towards Education, Equality and Social Justice at School Level

- *Elementary Level:* The Government of India has initiated a number of policy interventions with a view to ensuring equality and social justice at elementary level of education. These programmes lay special emphasis on the education of SCs, STs, Girls and Minorities. The Government of India launched a nationwide Education for All (EFA) programme under the banner of 'Sarva Shiksha Abhiyan' (SSA) in 2001. The programme aims at providing eight years of contextually useful and quality elementary education to all the children in the age group of 6-14 by the year 2010. The programme which focuses on girls especially those belonging to SCs, STs and Minorities is committed to bridging both gender and social gaps in primary classes (I-V) by 2007 and in upper primary classes (VI-VIII) by 2010. In doing so, it is committed to ensuring universal retention by 2010 besides focusing on satisfactory quality (universal achievement) with emphasis on education for life. The targeted provisions for girls under SSA include:

- Free text books to all girls up to class VIII.
- Separate toilets for girls.
- Back to school camps for out-of-school girls.
- Bridge courses for older girls.
- Recruitment of 50 per cent women teachers.
- Early Childhood Care and Education Centres (ECCE) in/near schools/convergences with Integrated Child Development Services (ICDS) programme, etc.
- Gender-sensitive teaching-learning materials including textbooks.
- Intensive community mobilisation efforts.
- Innovation fund per district for need based interventions for ensuring girls' attendance and retention.

The Government of India has provided additional resources to implement two of its significant schemes, namely the schemes of National Programmes for Education of Girls at Elementary Level (NPEGEL) and the Kasturba Gandhi Balika Vidyalaya (KGBV). These schemes are specifically designed to reach out to girls from marginalised social groups in over 3,000 educationally backward blocks in the country where the female rural literacy is below and the gender gap in literacy is above the national average. The NPEGEL provides additional provisions for enhancing the education of underprivileged girls at elementary level through more intense community mobilisation, the development of model schools in clusters, gender sensitisation of teachers, development of gender sensitive learning materials, ECCE facilities and provision of need-based incentives like escorts, stationery, work books and uniforms, etc., for girls.

The KGBV is a scheme that was launched in July 2004 for setting up residential schools at upper primary level for girls belonging predominantly to the under-privileged sections of society, namely, SCs, STs, OBCs and Minority Communities. The scheme is being implemented in educationally backward blocks of the country where the female rural literacy is below and gender gap in literacy is above the national average. The scheme provides for a minimum reservation of 75 per cent of the seats for girls belonging to SCs, STs, OBCs and Minority Communities and priority for the remaining 25 per cent, is accounted to girls from families below poverty line.

For the education of SCs and STs, special interventions have been launched under SSA. They include supply of free text books and uniforms, remedial classes for improving the learning competency, development of instructional material in local dialect for ST children and training to the teachers at cluster resource centres and block resource centres on tribal pedagogy. In addition, the child tracking approach is also adopted in formal schools in the tribal areas so as to ensure that the children enrolled continue and complete their education.

All these initiatives at elementary stage have shown substantial progress on certain key indicators like access, enrolment, drop-out rates, transition rates and learning achievement. Access to schooling facilities among the most disadvantaged has improved remarkably. Enrolment in a single year 2006-07 has gone up by 3, 93,000 as compared to the previous year. Drop-out rates at primary have declined by 4.5 percentage points. There has been a reduction of 5 percentage points in girls' drop-out. The transition rates from primary to upper primary have gone up from 74.15 per cent in 2003-04 to

83.36 per cent in 2005-06. Student attendance and teacher attendance have also shown considerable improvement.

- *Secondary Level:* The demand for secondary education has increased manifold because of the success of SSA on the one hand and increased aspirations for post secondary education on the other. Access, equity and quality are three major challenges of secondary education. Having regard to that, the Government of India has introduced various schemes at the secondary level with a view to improving access, equity and quality.

Remedial and special coaching are provided to SC and ST students in classes IX-XII. While the remedial coaching aims at removing deficiencies in various subjects, the special coaching is provided with a view to preparing the students for competitive examinations for seeking entry into professional courses like engineering and medical disciplines. In certain States like Haryana and Maharashtra, the Governments under the welfare schemes also provide free uniforms, free text-books, free noon meals, free bus pass and free bicycles to all SC and ST girl students studying in XI and XII standards of government schools. Preference is given to educationally backward districts particularly those predominantly inhabited by SCs and STs and educationally backward minorities. Besides all these SC and ST students who live in hostels are provided a financial assistance at the rate of Rs. 400 per month for 10 months in a year on account of hostel charges.

In addition, the Government of India has established as many as 897 Kendriya Vidyalays (KVs) wherein 15 per cent seats are reserved for SCs and 7.5 per cent seats for STs and no tuition fee is charged from either of the two. Besides, the Government has also established 567 Jawahar Navodaya Vidyalayas (JNVs) almost one in each district. These are boarding schools imparting education from classes VI-XII. These institutions are based on the principles of equity coupled with excellence. In these schools, 75 per cent seats are meant for rural children while the remaining 25 per cent seats are meant for urban children. Reservation of seats in favour of children belonging to SCs and STs is provided in proportion to their population in the concerned district provided that in no district such reservation will be less than the national average (15% for SCs and 7.5% for STs) but subject to a maximum of 50 per cent for both the categories taken together. These reservations are inter-changeable. One third of total seats in these schools are filled in by girls.

During the 11th Plan, the Government is giving more emphasis on the expansion and quality improvement of secondary education. The major development programme envisaged to be implemented by the Central Government is named 'SUCCESS'. For making secondary education of satisfactory quality accessible to all, some of the strategic interventions include setting up of 6,000 high quality model schools at block level, upgrading of 15,000 existing primary schools to secondary schools, increasing the intake of existing secondary schools by about 44,000, strengthening existing infrastructure in existing schools, expansion of KVs and JNVs in under-served areas, more hostels for girls, SCs and STs and OBCs, establishment of girls secondary schools at block headquarters and in towns with more than 10,000 population, intensive use of Information and Communication Technology (ICT), etc.

Participation in Higher Education

Enrolment at Higher Education

The institutions of higher education during its initial years largely catered to the elite sections of the society. However, with the adoption of several policies towards inclusion and to diversify the intake of higher education institutions, the winds of change have blown in favour of marginalised social groups including women. The composition of student community began to change since independence. Now, one can find more number of girls and students from marginal groups on the campuses than what they used to be six decades ago.

The enrolment in higher education institutions has increased by 6 folds from 1.71 million to 10.16 million students between 1970-71 and 2005-06. The share of girls and marginal groups has also increased along with the expansion of higher education. The proportion of girls in enrolment at higher education level increased from 24 per cent in 1970-71 to 39 per cent in 2005-06. The affirmative policies like special scholarships, fee waivers, separate hostels, etc., for girls along with attitudinal change are responsible for these positive developments.

The marginal groups like SCs and STs are also beginning to enter the higher education system in large numbers. This may be attributed to several affirmative actions which the government has introduced in the form of reservations, scholarships, fee waivers, relaxation in minimum requirements for entry to these institutions. The proportion of SCs in enrolment at higher education has increased from 8.5 per cent in 1990-91 to 12.3 per cent in 2005-06 which is almost 4 percentage points lesser than their share in the total population. The proportion of STs in enrolment at higher education has increased from 2.1 per cent in 1990-91 to 4.3 per cent in 2005-06, which like SCs is almost 4 percentage points lesser than their share in the total population. It shows that though some ground has been covered but still their share in enrolment in higher education is less than their share in the total population. This is further confirmed by GER by social groups as discussed below. Further, it can also be noticed from the data that most of the students from marginal groups tend to concentrate in conventional areas of study. Their proportion in these disciplines corresponds to their share in the population. In hard subjects like engineering or research their share is of course much less than their corresponding share in population.

- *GER at Higher Education Level:* Though Indian higher education system is considered to be the largest system in terms of number of institutions but in relative terms only a small proportion of corresponding age population is enrolled in higher education. The data on GER at higher education level are available only for the last three years. The GER at higher education level increased from 9.2 per cent in 2003-04 to 11.6 per cent in 2005-06. The GER for girls is 9.4 per cent compared to 13.6 per cent for boys in 2005-06. Similarly the GER for SC girls is 6.4 per cent compared to 10.16 per cent for boys in 2005-06. The GER for ST girls is 4.69 per cent compared to 8.59 per cent for boys in 2005-06. It shows that the GER for girls is almost 4 percentage points lower than the GER for boys across various social groups. Concerted efforts are, therefore, required to close these gender gaps on the one hand and increase their participation rates on the other.

Interestingly the proportion of girls in enrolment in higher education is declining during the last three years. This is also reflected in gender parity index. It declined from 0.72 in 2003-04 to 0.69 in 2005-06 in respect of general candidates and from 0.64 in 2004-05 to 0.63 in respect of SCs between 2004-05 and 2005-06. The gender parity index, however, remains static in case of STs between 2004-05 and 2005-06. It is difficult to guess the reasons for the same. It may be merely an error in data reporting or a reflection of structural changes such as increasing privatisation in the recent past.

Policy Interventions towards Equality and Social Justice at Higher Education Level

From time to time the Government of India has launched a number of schemes and programmes for the purposes of enhancing the participation of deprived classes in higher education. India has about 21.092 institutions of higher learning including universities, institutes of national importance and colleges. The Government has made it mandatory for all these institutions to provide 15 per cent reservation to SCs, 7.5 per cent reservation to STs. In addition, the Central Government has now provided for 27 per cent reservation to OBCs in all centrally funded institutions of higher learning. Apart from reservation, there is also a relaxation given in the minimum qualifying marks for admission for these children. Besides, seats are also reserved in hostels for these children. These measures are certainly going to make substantial improvement in the participation level of underprivileged sections of the society in higher education.

The SC/ST students who secure admission in the notified institutions are given scholarship to meet the requirements for full tuition fees, living expenses, books and stationery. The scholarship once awarded continues till the completion of the course, subject to satisfactory performance. Under the 'Book Bank Scheme' the SC and ST students pursuing Medical, Engineering, Agriculture, Veterinary, Polytechnics, Law, Chartered Accountancy, MBA and Bio-Sciences courses are also provided books. The Scheme provides for sharing of text books by two students at undergraduate level and separate set of books at Post-Graduate level. Students with disabilities amongst SCs and STs are also provided specified special allowances like readers allowance, transport allowance, escort allowance etc. Not only that the Government of India provides 17 overseas scholarships each year to the meritorious SC and ST students who wish to pursue higher studies abroad. The SC and ST students pursuing higher education are also provided free remedial coaching to enable them to upgrade their merit. Besides, they are also provided free coaching for entry into services.

In order to provide relevant and good quality higher education in an equitable manner the Government has proposed a number of measures to remove regional, social and gender disparities. The government proposes to establish 370 new colleges in districts with GER less than national average, 14 world class universities and 16 Central Universities in hitherto uncovered states. The government has also committed to provide increased financial assistance to institutions located in border, hilly, remote and educationally backward areas. The central government is also going to provide increased support to institutions with large percentage of SC, ST, OBC, girls and minority population. Besides, the government is also committed to build more hostels for the students belonging to underprivileged sections of the society.

Major Challenges and way Forward

Elementary Education

Every country develops its system of education to express and promote its unique socio-cultural identity and also to meet the challenges of the times. The catalytic action of education in this complex and dynamic growth process needs to be planned meticulously and executed with great sensitivity. This has all the more significance for a country like India with a plural culture and a concern for an egalitarian society.

Though India has made monumental progress in elementary education both in quantitative and qualitative terms, there still remains a wide gap between supply and demand because of its number and vastness. The biggest challenge before the country is to bring in all the children into the fold of elementary schooling as also to increasing the internal efficiency of its schools. This would warrant a number of complementary engagements like increasing the intake capacity of existing institutions, setting up of new institutions, ensuring competent and qualified teachers in each classroom, reinventing curriculum, introduction of appropriate pedagogy, implementation of continuous and comprehensive evaluation, increasing the number of learners with increased learning, improving the transition rate from lower primary to upper primary, creating equal opportunities for accessing elementary schooling, bridging gender and social gaps, reducing dropout rates, providing research based interventions in backward areas, mobilisation of public resources, etc.

- *Secondary Education:* The challenges of secondary education are much more daunting as this sector has always been sandwiched between elementary education because of constitutional obligation towards EFA and higher education because of its potential for creating higher level expertise in knowledge areas. The principal challenge is to increase access to secondary education besides creating equal opportunities for accessing secondary schooling facilities in backward areas.

Another huge challenge is to upgrade and rationalise infrastructure and teaching learning facilities of existing institutions on the basis of given norms. The country will also have to undertake school mapping exercise with a view to ensuring the requirements of existing schools and opening of new institutions. Teacher preparation, meeting additional teacher requirements and professional development of teachers will be another big challenge. Equity concerns with regard to gender, social groups and minority communities acquire a bigger dimension at secondary stage as this would warrant special interventions in terms of differential treatment to ensure both participation and success of one and all. Special attention will have to be paid to upgrade and diversify the curriculum to make it more relevant in today's context. Yet other challenges in secondary education are integration of ICT in all public institutions, expansion of open and distance learning facilities and building district and sub-district data base.

- *Higher Education:* Despite being the largest system of higher education in terms of number of institutions, the access ratio in India is still lower (12%) than the average of the developing nations (13%). Therefore, major challenge in higher education is to increase the access ratio to a minimum threshold of 20 per cent. This would mean optimizing the existing institutions and creating new facilities, more so in backward areas to make higher education more inclusive. The pace of affirmative action ought to be accelerated to ensure larger participation of SCs, STs, Women and minority students in progressive disciplines. The initiatives like scholarships, hostels, special coaching for students belonging to marginal classes must be further strengthened. Increasing tuition fees beyond a certain level may lead to regressive effects and deprive the children of the under privileged classes from accessing higher education. Responding to the specific economic and academic needs of the first generation entrants to higher education is yet another major challenge. Therefore, the public funding will have to be increased manifold. Besides, privatisation of higher education in the recent past has led to commercialisation which has made an adverse impact not only on access and equity but also on the overall development of higher education. Foreign institutions, which have been operating in a variety of ways, have also contributed to commercialisation. Therefore, the biggest challenge for the government is to come up with appropriate regulations to contain the menace of commercialisation and at the same time to ensure the co-existence of both public and private systems. The privatisation and internationalisation of higher education should not be allowed to create a wedge between different sections of the society. Distance education is yet another area which ought to be properly regulated in terms of its quality and cost. Other major challenges include promotion of research and its integration with teaching, industry-academia collaboration, successful implementation of affirmative actions for the promotion of deprived sections, granting autonomy, periodic assessment and accreditation of institutions, use of ICT in higher education, development of educational management information system, etc.

REFERENCE

1. Prakash, Ved. (2008), Education, Equality and Social Justice: An Indian Scenario. Paper to be Presented in the II International Symposium and Public Forum on "Education, Equality and Social Justice" Organized in Brasilia and Campo Grande, from April 22 - 27, 2008. Downloaded from http://www.wordwendang.com

Bibliography

1. —— (1986), National Policy on Education, 1986, Government of India, New Delhi.
2. —— (1966), Report of the Education Commission 1964-66: Education and National Development. Delhi: Government of India.
3. —— (1978), The II Backward Classes Commission, 1978 (Mandal Commission), New Delhi.
4. —— (1992), National Policy on Education, 1986 (Revised 1992), Government of India, New Delhi.
5. —— (2001), C-series Tables on Scheduled Castes, 2001, Government of India, New Delhi.
6. —— (2006), Social, Economic and Educational Status of the Muslim Community of India, (Chair: Justice R. Sachar), Prime Minister's High Level Committee, Cabinet Secretariat, Government of India, New Delhi.
7. —— (Various Years), Annual Report, Government of India, New Delhi. 20 21.
8. A Compilation of Notes on Common School System by Prof. Anil Sadgopal Presented at the Meeting of CABE at New Delhi in July 2005.

9. Agarwal, P. (2006), "Higher education in India: The Need for Change". Working Paper No. 180. *Indian Council for Research on International Economic Relations*.
10. Aggaral, J.C. (2003), *Teacher and Education in a Developing Society*. New Delhi: Vikas Publishing House (P) Ltd.
11. Aggarwal, J.C. (1992), *Theory and Principles of Education*. New Delhi: Vikas Publishing House (P) Ltd.
12. Aggarwal, J.C. (1995), *Teacher and Education in a Developing Society*. New Delhi: Vikas Publishing House Pvt. Ltd.
13. Aggarwal, J.C. (2003), *Development and Planning of Modern Education*. New Delhi: Vikas Publishing House (P.) Ltd.
14. Ahuja, B.N. and Bhatia, R.L. (2004), *Modern Indian Education and Its Problems*. Delhi: Surjeet Publications.
15. Alston, P. and Bhuta, N., (2005), Human Rights and Public Goods: Education as a Fundamental Right in India, Centre for Human Rights and Global Justice Working Paper, Economic, Social and Cultural Rights Series, Number 5.
16. Amala, Annie, *et al.* (2006), *History of Education*. New Delhi: Discovery Publishing House.
17. B. C. Rai (1997), *Theory of Education – Sociological and Philosophical Bases and Education*. Lucknow: Prakashan Kendra.
18. Bakshi, P. M. (2003), The Constitution of India, Universal Law Publishing Co. Pvt. Ltd. Delhi.
19. Basu, D. D., *Introduction to the Constitution of India*.
20. Belock and Green, J. L., *Philosophy and Education*. Meerut: Any Prakashan.
21. Beteille, A. (2000), "The Scheduled Castes: An Inter-Regional Perspective", in A. Beteille (ed.), *Journal of Indian School of Political Economy*, 12 (3 and 4): 367-80.
22. Bhatia, K. K. *et al.*, *Modern Indian Education and Its Problems*. Ludhyana: Tandon Publishers.
23. Bhatt, B. D. and Sharma, S. R. (1993), *Sociology of Education*. New Delhi: Kanishka Publishing House.

24. Bhatt, G. D (2005), *Educational Development of Scheduled Castes*, Himalayan Region Study and Research Institute, Delhi.

25. Bhattacharya, S. (1996), *Foundations of Education*. New Delhi: Atlantic Publishers and Distributors.

26. Botia, B. and Bhatia, K. (1992), *The Philosophical and Sociological Foundations of Education*. New Delhi: Doaba House.

27. Bourai, H. H. A. (1993), *Indian Theory of Education*. New Delhi: B. R. Publishing Corp.

28. Butler, J. D. (1966), *Idealism in Education*. New York: Harper and Row.

29. CABE: Report on the Universalisation of Secondary Education (June, 2005).

30. Census of India (2001), Provisional Population Tables, Series 1, India, Paper 1, 2001, Web Edition, New Delhi.

31. Chakraborty, A. K. (2003), *Principle and Practice of Education*. Meerat: R. Lal Book Depot.

32. Chandra, S. S. and Sharma, R. (1996), *Philosophy of Education*. New Delhi: Atlantic Publishers.

33. Chandra, S. S. (2003), *Adult and Non-Formal Education*. New Delhi: Surjeet Publishers.

34. Chaube, S. P. and Chaube, A. (1987), *Foundations of Education*. New Delhi: Vikas Publishing House (P) Ltd.

35. Chaube, S. P. *History and Problems of Indian Education*. Agra: Vinod Pustakmandir.

36. Chaube, S. P. *History of Indian Education*. Agra: Vinod Pustak Mandir.

37. Colclough, C., and De, A., 2010, The Impact of Aid on Education Policy in India, *International Journal of Educational Development*, 30/5: 497-507.

38. Conner D. J. O. (1957), *An Introduction to the Philosophy of Education*. London: Routledge Kegan Paul.

39. Dr. R. C. Bhardwaj, *Constitution Amendment in India*.

40. C. K. Jain, *Constitution of India*.

41. Das, P. N. (2004, May), *Mathrubhumi Thozhil Wartha*, p. 36.
42. Dasgupta, Partha and David, Paul A. (1994), 'Towards a New Economics of Science'. Research Policy, Vol. 23, No. 5, pp. 487-521.
43. *Development of Indian System of Education*. Dr. Ramashakal Pandey.
44. Dreze, J., and Goyal, A., (2003), Future of Mid-Day Meals, MPRA Paper No. 17386, Available at: http://mpra.ub.uni-muenchen.de/17386/ [Accessed on 10th November 2009].
45. *Encyclopaedia of Sociology* (Vol. I) – Laxmi Devi.
46. Entwistle, Harold (1997), *Class, Culture and Education*. London: New Fetter Lane.
47. Fennell, S., 2006. Future Policy Choices for the Education Sector in Asia, Paper 3, Parallel Group 3B, Session 3, *Asia 2015 Conference on Promoting Growth, Ending Poverty*, DFID, London, March 2006.
48. Fennell, S., (2007), Tilting at Windmills: Public Private Partnerships in Indian Education Today, RECOUP Working Paper No. 5, University of Cambridge.
49. Fennell, S., (2010), *Rules, Rubrics and Riches: the Relationship between Law, Institutions and International Development*, Abingdon and New York: Routledge.
50. Ganesh, K. N., (2005), National Curriculum Framework 2005: A Note, *Social Scientist*, 33 (9/10), 47-54.
51. Ganta, R. and Dash, B.N. (2005), *Foundations of Education*. Hyderabad: Neelkamal Publishers (P) Ltd.
52. Gerald L. Gutek. *Philosophical and Ideological Perspectives on Education*.
53. Gerald, C. G. *Philosophical and Ideological Perspectives of Education*
54. Ghanta, Ramesh and Dash, B.N. (2006), *Foundations of Education*. Hyderabad: Neelkamal Pub (P) Ltd.
55. Government of India (1955), The Backward Classes Commission, 1955 (Kelkar Commission), Volumes 3, New Delhi.

56. Government of India, (2005a), *CABE Committee on Regulatory Mechanisms for Textbooks and Parallel Textbooks Taught in Schools Outside the Government System*, Ministry of Human Resource Development, New Delhi: India.
57. Government of India, (2005b), *Report of the CABE Committee on Girls' Education and the Common School System*, Ministry of Human Resource Development, New Delhi: India.
58. Government of India, (2005c), *Report of the CABE Committee on Universalisation of Secondary Education*, Ministry of Human Resource Development, New Delhi: India.
59. Government of India, (2005d), *Report of the Central Advisory Board of Education (CABE) Committee on Autonomy of Higher Education Institutions*, Ministry of Human Resource Development, Department of Secondary and Higher Education, New Delhi: India.
60. Government of India, (2005e), *Report of the Central Advisory Board of Education (CABE) Committee on Free and Compulsory Education Bill and Other Issues Relating to Elementary Education*, Ministry of Human Resource Development, New Delhi: India.
61. Government of India. (2005f), The Millennium Development Goals Country Report, 2005. New Delhi, Government of India.
62. Habib, I., (2005), How to Evade Real Issues and Make Room for Obscurantism, *Social Scientist*, 33 (9/10), 3-12.
63. Hospers, John (1953), *An Introduction to Philosophical Analysis*. London: Prentice Hall.
64. http://groupsgoogle.co.in/group/bangalore
65. http://mhrd.gov.in
66. http://planningcommission.nic.in/sectors/index.php?sectors=edu
67. http://rehabcouncil.nic.in/index.htm
68. http://www.education.nic.in/secedu/sec_iedc.asp
69. http://www.education.nic.in/secedu/sec_iedc.asp

70. http://www.google.co.in/search?hl=en&q=inclusive+education+issues+and+intervention&meta=cr%3DcountryIN&aq=f&oq=

71. http://www.ias.ac.in/academy/misc_docs/sci_edu-insa_ias.pdf

72. http://www.uis.unesco.org/profiles/EN/EDU/country Profile_en.aspx?code=3560. [Downloaded 10th February 2010]

73. ID 21 – Communicating Development Research – Approaches to Inclusive Education.

74. Ismail Thamarasseri (2007), *Education in the Emerging Indian Society*. New Delhi: Kanishka Publishers.

75. Ismail Thamarasseri (2008), *Early Childhood and Elementary Education*. New Delhi: Kanishka Publishers.

76. Ismail Thamarasseri (2013), *Philosophical Foundations of Education*. Agra: Sri Vinod Pustak Mandir.

77. J. P. Naik., *The Role of Government of India in Education*. Government of India: Ministry of Education.

78. Jayaraman, R., (2008), The Impact of School Lunches on Enrolment: Evidence from an Exogenous Policy Change in India, Available from; http://www.client.norc.org/jole/SOLEweb/9001.pdf [Accessed 20th March 2010].

79. Jeffery, C. P. Jeffery and R. Jeffery (2005), 'Broken Trajectories: Dalit Young Mend and Formal Eduation', in Radhika Chopra and Patricia Jeffery (Eds.) *Educational Regimes in Contemporary India*, pp. 256-275, Konrad Adenauer Stiftung and Sage, New Delhi.

80. Jeffery, C. P. Jeffery and R. Jeffery (2005), Reproducing Difference? Schooling, Jobs, and Empowerement in Uttar Pradesh, India' *World Development* Vol. 33, No. 12, pp. 2085-2101.

81. Jha, P. *et.al.* (2008), *Public Provisioning for Elementary Education*, New Delhi: Sage.

82. Kamala Bhatia and Baldev Bhatia (1992), *The Philosophical and Sociological Foundations of Education*. New Delhi: Doaba House.

83. Kashyap C.S. (2005), *Our Constitution – An Introduction to India's Constitution and Constitutional Law*. New Delhi: National Book Trust, India.

84. Khera, R., M. Samon and A. De, (2009), Incentives that Work, *The Hindu*, May 10, 2009.

85. Kneller, G.F. (1971), *Introduction to the Philosophy of Education*. New York: John Willy and Sons.

86. Kornblum, William (1998), *Sociology the Central Themes*. New York: Harcourt Brace College Publishers.

87. Koul, Lokesh (1997), *Methodology of Educational Research*. New Delhi: Vikas Publishing House, Pvt. Ltd.

88. Koushik, V. K. and Ravi, Prakash (1996), *A Sociology of Educating – Teaching and Curriculum*. New Delhi: Kanishka Publishers.

89. Krishnamurti Foundation India (1991), *Krishnamurti to Himself His Last Journal*. Madras: Auther.

90. Kumar, K., (2004), Quality of Education at the Beginning of the 21st Century: Lessons from India, Background Paper for the Education For All Global Monitoring Report 2005, *The Quality Imperative*.

91. *Land Marks in the History of Modern Indian Education* – J. C. Aggarwal.

92. *Learning without Burdon* – Report of the National Advisory Committee Appointed by MHRD, Government of India.

93. M. Niaz Asadullah and Gaston Yalonetzky. (August 2010), *Inequality of Educational Opportunity in India: Changes over Time and across States*. Germany: IZA DP No. 5146.

94. Manuel, N.V., *Reading and Challenges in Philosophy of Education*. Unpublished Material.

95. Mathur, S.S. *A Sociological Approach to Indian Education*, Agra: Vinod Pustak Mandir.

96. Meigham, Roland (1996), *A Sociology of Educating*. London: Cassell Educational Ltd.

97. Ministry of Human Resource Development (2005), Report of the Committee on National Common Minimum

Programme's Commitment of Six Per cent of GDP to Education, NIEPA, New Delhi.

98. Ministry of Human Resource Development (Various Years), Selected Educational Statistics, Government of India, New Delhi.
99. Ministry of Human Resource Development (Various Years), *Selected Educational Statistics*, MHRD, New Delhi.
100. Ministry of Human Resource Development, (2004), Resolution on the Reconstitution of the CABE, June 2004.
101. Ministry of Social Justice and Empowerment (2006), Annual Report, 2005-06, Government of India, New Delhi.
102. Mishra B.C (1996), Education of Tribal Children, Discovery Publishing House, New Delhi.
103. Monroe, Paul (2001), *Encyclopaedia of Philosophy of Education*. New Delhi: Cosmo Publications.
104. Mooij, J., (2007), Is There an Indian Policy Process?: An Investigation into Two Social Processes, *Social Policy and Administration*, 4 (4) 323-338.
105. Murty, S.K. (1992), *Contemporary Problems and Current Trends in Education*. Ludhiana: Parkash Brothers.
106. Nanda, S.K. (2000), *Indian Education and its Problems Today*. New Delhi: Kalyani Publishers.
107. National Commission for Scheduled Castes and Scheduled Tribes, Sixth Report, 1999-2000 and 2000-01, Government of India, New Delhi.
108. National Family Health Survey (NFHS-3) India, 2005-06.
109. NSSO (2006), Employment and Unemployment Situation among Social Groups in India, 2004-05, NSS, 61st Round (July 2004-June 2005), Report No. 516.
110. Padma Velaskar (2006), National Commitment to Education of the Dalits: A Critical Commentary on the Report of the Education Commission (1964-66) Paper presented at National Seminar on "The Education Commission: Revisiting the Commission's Premises,

Vision and Impact on Policy Formulation" organized by NUEPA, 26-28 December 2006, New Delhi.

111. Pandey, R. S. (1991), *A Survey of Educational Thought*. Allahabad: Horizon Publishers.

112. Pandey, Ramshakal. *Teacher in Developing Indian Society*. Agra: Vinod Pustakmandir.

113. Pathak, C.K. (2003), *Adult Education – Millennium Challenges*. New Delhi: Rajat Publishers.

114. Prakash Ved (2007), Higher Education in India: Growth and the Diversity of Expectations. Revue Internationale D'Éducation – Sèvres No 45 – September 2007.

115. Prakash Ved (2007), Trends in Growth and Financing of Higher Education in India, *Economic and Political Weekly*, August 4, 2007.

116. Prakash, Ved. (2008), Education, Equality and Social Justice: An Indian Scenario. Paper to be Presented in the II International Symposium and Public Forum on "Education, Equality and Social Justice" Organized in Brasilia and Campo Grande, from April 22-27, 2008. Downloaded from http://www.wordwendang.com

117. Pritchett, L., and V. Pande, (2006), Making Primary Education Work for India's Poor: A Proposal for Effective Decentralisation, Social Development Department, South Asia Series, No. 95, June 2006.

118. Pylee, M.V. (2003), *Indian Constitution*. Thiruvananthapuram: Kerala Bhasha Institute.

119. Pylee, M.V. (2005), *An Introduction to the Constitution of India*. New Delhi: Vikas Publishing House (P) Ltd.

120. Rai, B.C. (1997), *Sociological and Philosophical Theory of Education*. Lucknow: Prakashan Kendra.

121. Raina, V. 2008, Right to Education, *Seminar*, 15th December 2008.

122. Ramachandran, V., (2004), *Gender and Social Equity in Primary Education: Hierarchies of Access*, New Delhi: Sage.

123. Rao Bhaskara N and Kulkarni Suresh Disparities in School Facilities in India: The Case of Scheduled Castes and

Scheduled Tribe Children. *Journal of Educational Planning and Administration,* Vol. XII, Number 2, April 1999.

124. Rao, D. B. (Ed) (2003), *Teachers in a Changing World*. New Delhi: Discovery Publishing House.
125. Rao, V. K. (1999), *Vocational Education*. New Delhi: Rajat Publishers.
126. Reeba, K.R. (2002), *Educational Contributions of Jiddu Krishnamurthi*. Unpublished P.G. Dissertation, Mahatma Gandhi University, Kottayam.
127. Roand Meigham. *A Sociology of Educating*.
128. Robert R. Rusk. *The Philosophical Base of Education*. University of London Press.
129. Ruhela, S. P. *India's Struggle to Universalize Elementary Education*.
130. Sachdev, Menraj (n.a.), 'The social Perspective's of India's Higher Education System'. Faculty of Education and Social Work, University of Sydney. www.aare.edu.au/04pap/sac04343.pdf.
131. Sadgopal, A., (2005), A Compilation of Notes on the Common School System, Presented at the Meeting of the Central Advisory Board of Education on 14-15th July 2005.
132. Sadgopal, A., (2005b), On the Pedagogy of Writing a National Curricular Framework: Some Reflections From an Insider, *Social Scientist*, 3 (9/10), 23-36.
133. Samson, M. Noronha, C. and De, A., (2007), Towards More Benefits from Delhi's Midday Meal Scheme, CORD, New Delhi.
134. Sarangapani, P., (2003), *Constructing School Knowledge: An Ethnography of Learning in an Indian Village*, New Delhi: Sage.
135. Sataya, Raghunath. (1993), *New Thoughts on Education*. Ambala: The Indian Publications.
136. Saxena, S. N. R. (2006), *Foundation of Educational Thought and Practice*. Meerut: R. Lall Book Depot.

137. *School Education in 1990's* – NCERT Publication.

138. Shailaja Fennell (October 2010), *Educational Exclusion and Inclusive Development in India*. Dept of International Development. Research Consortium on Educational Outcomes and Poverty.

139. Sharma, R. (2000), *Text-book of Educational Philosophy*. New Delhi: Kanishka Publishers.

140. Sharma, R. K. and Chandra, S.S. (1996), *Principles of Education*. New Delhi: Atlantic Publishers and Distributors.

141. Sharma, R. N. (2000), *Text-book of Educational Philosophy*. New Delhi: Kanishka Publications.

142. Sharma, R. N. *History and Problems of Education in India*. New Delhi: Surjeet Publications.

143. Sharma, S. R. (1997), *Practice of Philosophy of Education*. New Delhi: Mohit Publications.

144. Sharma, Y. K. (2003), *The Doctrines of the Great Indian Educators*. New Delhi: Kanishka Publishers.

145. Shivarajan. K. (2006), *Education in the Emerging Indian Society*. Calicut University Central Co-operative Stores.

146. Srinibas Bhattacharya (1996), *Foundation of Education*. New Delhi: Atlantic Publishers.

147. *Subhrajit Sinha, Development Support, CRY. subhrajit.sinha@crymail.org*

148. Sunita Kishor and Kamla Gupta (August 2009), Gender Equality and Women's Empowerment in India. Ministry of Health and Family Welfare, Government of India.

149. Taneja, R. P. (2000), *Dictionary of Education*. Anmol Publishing Ltd.

150. Taneja, V. P. (2003), *Educational Thought and Practice*. New Delhi: Sterling Publishers (P) Ltd.

151. *Teacher and Education in Indian Society* – by Dr. K.V. Eapen.

152. Tilak, J., (2009), Universalising Elementary Education: A Review of Progress, Policies and Problems, in P. Rustagi, ed. *Concerns, Conflicts, and Cohesions:*

Universalisation of Elementary Education in India, New Delhi: Oxford University Press.

153. UNESCO, (2008), Global Monitoring Report: Education For All: Will We Make It? Oxford and New York: Oxford University Press.
154. UNESCO, 2008. UIS. Available at:
155. Vekateswaran, S. (1993), *Principles of Education*. New Delhi: Vikas Publishing House (P) Ltd.
156. Venkataiah, S. (2002), *Vocational Education*. New Delhi: Anmol Publishers (P) Ltd.
157. Vidya Bushan and Sachdeva (1995), *An Introduction to Sociology*. Allahabad: Kitab Mahal.
158. World Bank (2001a and 2001b), 'Constructing Knowledge Societies: New Challenges for Tertiary Institutions, Volumes I and II.' Draft paper, Education Group: Human Development Network, World Bank.
159. www.cde.ca.gov.
160. www.edu.gov.
161. www.indg.in/primary-education/policiesandschemes/right-to-education-bill
162. www.oneworld.net
163. Yogendra, K. S. (2006), *History and Problems of Education*. New Delhi: Kanishka Publishers.

Index